violence
in America

violence
in America

Lessons on Understanding the Aggression in Our Lives

Arnold P. Goldstein

Davies-Black Publishing
Palo Alto, California

Published by Davies-Black Publishing, an imprint of Consulting Psychologists Press, Inc., 3803 East Bayshore Road, Palo Alto, California 94303; 1-800-624-1765.

Special discounts on bulk quantities of Davies-Black Publishing books are available to corporations, professional associations, and other organizations. For details, contact the Director of Book Sales at Davies-Black Publishing, 3803 East Bayshore Road, Palo Alto, California 94303; 415-691-9123; Fax 415-988-0673.

The quotation in the essay "The Costs of Aggression Are Huge, and We All Pay" is reprinted with permission of Research Press, from *Break It Up: A Teacher's Guide to Managing Student Aggression*, Arnold P. Goldstein et al., 1995.

Quotations in the essay "Voices From Prison" are reprinted with permission from *Prison Life* magazine.

The essay "Raising Children to Resist Violence" is reprinted with permission from the American Psychological Association and from the American Academy of Pediatrics.

This book was printed using Soy Ink™, a soy-based ink.

99 98 97 96   10 9 8 7 6 5 4 3 2 1
Printed in the United States of America

Library of Congress Cataloging-in-Publication Data
Goldstein, Arnold P.
     Violence in America : lessons on understanding the aggression in our
lives / Arnold P. Goldstein.   —   1st ed.
         p.   cm.
     Paperback ISBN 0-89106-092-8
     Hardback ISBN 0-89106-086-3
     1. Violence—United States. 2. Violent crimes—United States.
I. Title.
HN90.V5G63   1996
303.6'0973—dc20   96-21541
                                                                        CIP
FIRST EDITION
First printing 1996

*To the blue flag, the yellow ribbon, the white feather,
and the solstice tree*

Contents

Preface

This is a book about violence in America, about the aggression in our lives, homes, streets, schools, and elsewhere. Its pages speak to our hates, our fights, our anger, the crimes we commit and those in which we are victims. It is a book about us, strangers, your neighbors, you, me, all of us.

Violence in America is both our business and our hobby, our preoccupation and our pastime. It fills our thoughts and our reality. Our media portray it, our papers report it, our citizens commit it, and in this book we try to better understand it. We will consider its many forms, both criminal and otherwise; its costs and motivations; its perpetrators and targets; its likely and unlikely locations; its impact on our children, our schools, our marriages, and our hopes; and, most especially, its several causes and promising solutions.

Topics of special interest include violence and the challenge of raising children; aggression in our classrooms; American youth gangs; life in our prisons; past and future sports violence; "hot spot" locations of frequent violence; and the aggression-promoting role of alcohol, temperature, driving cars, television, and other features of modern life. The book also deals with such questions as, Is aggression always bad? How do aggressive thoughts lead to aggressive actions? Is aggression, at least for some people, an addiction? Is there such a thing as violent death by imitation? Do victims contribute to being attacked? Is dating a dangerous game? Should we be more worried now than in the past about a possible presidential assassination? Are torturers ordinary or extraordinary people? How are acts of aggression committed in other countries and how are they dealt with? Any lessons for America?

A small number of core ideas characterize and tie together the essays that constitute this book. First is the growing pervasiveness of serious aggression in our lives today as it intrudes into our thoughts and affects our behavior. A connected theme concerns its sources and our data-based belief that for the most part aggression is not inborn but learned. This theme is a hopeful one, since anything learned can be unlearned, and alternatives—perhaps more peaceable—can emerge.

Yet they will only emerge with difficulty. The book's third central notion stresses just how resistant to change violent behavior is. Because it works so well, so often, in getting its perpetrator what he or she wants, it is not easily reduced. Fortunately, in recent years, means for seeking such aggression reduction have been put forth, tested, revised, and urged upon many of the chronically hostile, angry, or violent in our society. I will share these methods in detail, as well as emphasize that aggression control and reduction can go forward in a humane and constructive manner, without ever-greater reliance on severe punishment, a solution to which too many are turning today.

A syndrome such as violence is a set of actions or behaviors that form a pattern. From our beginnings as a nation, and evermore today, the violence syndrome is a major American pattern. Hand in hand with our charity, creativity, industry, and goodwill in dealing with one another are high levels of hostility, argumentativeness, abuse, assault, rape, and murder. I share here my thoughts and observations about such expressions of violence, in order to shed light on their nature and promote means for their reduction. Yes, we suffer badly from the violence syndrome, but its presence and pains are not inevitable. Violence can be understood, controlled, reduced, and often even eliminated. It is in this spirit and toward these goals that I have written this book

My thirty-five years as a clinical psychology and special education professor at Syracuse University, director of its Center for Research on Aggression, and practitioner of anger control and prosocial behavior training methods with literally thousands of aggressive youngsters and adults has armed me well for the reflective effort this book represents. In laboratory and street, home and prison, school and community, I have seen violence up close and personal. I have also seen and helped evaluate many dozens of attempts to moderate, control, reduce, and even eliminate such behavior. Our own research and that of my many colleagues has most certainly been helpful in furthering my own understanding of the complex, unpredictable, and dangerous behavior called violence. But even more so, I have learned major lessons and gathered a deeper sense of the nature of violence from thousands of hours spent talking to its victims and perpetrators, as well as to community caretakers in schools, prisons, and elsewhere who are working hard and often unappreciated to help us have fewer of both. I have tried to capture, build upon, and share this collective wisdom in the pages that follow. My aim is to apply the insights of psychology to a better understanding of what violence is and why it occurs and especially to aid the reader in preventing it entirely or moderating both its intensity and its consequences in their own lives. It is my hope that such greater understanding and more skilled efforts at prevention will substantially reduce America's long-standing and highly damaging violence syndrome.

1.

facts, figures, fictions, and realities

Aggression in America: Past and Present

An Introduction to Violence in Our Society

How Did We Get Here?

the United States was born in a spirit of freedom and democracy, yet also with a strong belief in the use of individual and group violence. The Revolutionary War lasted seven years and succeeded in its goal of a new and independent nation. It also began our two-century-long love affair with the gun, as four hundred thousand victorious citizen-soldiers helped proclaim the right to bear arms.

The new nation lay along the Eastern coast of a three-thousand-mile wide unexplored continent of buffalo and other game to kill, of Native Americans to displace, of a frontier to conquer. As our citizens began moving westward in the late 1700s, a frontier mentality went with them. Self-reliance, independence, and impatience with the poorly developed laws and law enforcement of the day were also part of this mentality. Justice often meant "frontier justice," in which groups of local citizenry took the law into their own hands: Hanging horse thieves or riding undesirables out of town were among the ways such early criminal sentencing was handled.

Though our mass media have long glamorized it, frontier living was rarely as easy and romantic as usually portrayed. Often, it was very difficult economically, which helped give rise to outlaw gangs, bank robbers, counterfeiters, and other criminal behavior. A tide of immigration to the United States commenced in earnest in the early 1800s, and grew to a flood of newcomers of diverse backgrounds to our shores as the twentieth century unfolded. The ingredients in this great, human melting pot often mixed poorly and often resulted in high levels of individual and group violence directed at these migrants, especially in the cities.

The Civil War, 1861 to 1865, pitted Northerner against Southerner and, at times, neighbor against neighbor, even cousin against cousin in bitter, lethal combat. Its price was high—well beyond the actual war casualties of 617,000 dead and 375,000 injured soldiers. Out of the war grew forces that yielded new and virulent forms of aggression throughout the country. Often stemming from war-related animosities, feuding, lynching, and high levels of vigilante activity erupted. The feud, primarily developing in Southern mountain states, was a kind of interfamily guerrilla warfare. Much more deadly in its effects was lynching, in which unorganized mobs captured and hung usually guiltless Black persons. It is the shame of America that 3,209 recorded lynchings occurred during the years 1889 to 1918.

Vigilante aggression also became more organized during this post–Civil War period, with the Ku Klux Klan, the Bald Knobbers, the White Cappers, and many more such groups targeting not just Blacks but several other minority groups as well. Also at this time, the much-romanticized cowboy gang became prominent. Their specialties, stagecoach, train, and bank robberies, although to this day portrayed as exciting and heroic events, were plain and simple acts of criminal violence.

Much of the recorded violence in America in the late 1800s and early 1900s was group violence associated with the industrialization of our country. There were violent labor strikes in the mining, railroad, and auto industries as well as violent government response to the strikers. Though there are numerous accounts of violence by individuals during these years, actual numbers are largely unavailable because the F.B.I. did not begin compiling crime statistics for murder, assault, rape, and similar violent crimes until 1933. Nevertheless, it is clear that during the years in which Prohibition was the law of the land (1920 to 1933), murder and mayhem between and among bootleggers and liquor highjackers in their rivalry for market control was at a level of often lethal intensity. During the two world wars and the economic depression in the 1930s, there was less violence here for individuals and groups. The same was true in other countries. Perhaps when citizens feel joined together against a common enemy, there is less motivation to attack each other.

As the twentieth century moved along, feuding, vigilante groups, lynching, and labor violence all receded, but aggression in seemingly new and more serious individual forms appeared. Spouse and child abuse had been with us all along but was in a sense "discovered" as it became a matter for more public discussion and concern in the mid-1960s. It has since become recognized as widely practiced in our homes and severely damaging to many of our citizens. So too for the crime of rape, as the women's movement of this same period called our collective attention to its nature, its frequency, and its serious consequences. As is widely known, in this period, America's homicide rate far exceeded that of all other modern nations—and still does today.

Since the 1970s, the levels of murder, rape, abuse, and assault by adults are a continuing serious concern, but our main worry seems to be the flourishing of juvenile crime. Aided by the massive influx of drugs into our country, armed by our arsenal of weaponry, encouraged by its unremitting portrayal in the media, and in imitation of many of their heroes, our sons and daughters have reached new peaks of aggression in their lives, both as individuals and in growing numbers of gangs.

So America's history is contradictory. We are a free, democratic, progressive, creative country of protected citizen rights, rule by law, legal transfer of power, economic opportunity for at least most of our citizens, and much more that is good. We are also a country in which for more than two hundred years our people have insulted, injured, assaulted, abused, raped, and murdered one another at levels that are dismayingly high and seem to be growing. That is where we are and, briefly, how we got here.

The Costs of Aggression
Are Huge, and We All Pay

1994, the cost of rape in the United States was approximately 14 billion dollars; robbery, 36 billion; aggravated assault, 123 billion. At first glance, such numbers seem like wild overestimates. True, we have much crime in our country, but certainly its expense cannot be even close to such figures!

These numbers, however, start to look a great deal more reasonable when we list specific costs. Victims of such violent crimes as rape, armed robbery, and aggravated assault incur many financial costs: the loss of cash or property; lost wages; lost productivity at work, school, or home; medical care; legal services; mental health services; and insurance.

But it is not only the victim who pays; we all do. The several costs to our communities for such violence include police and investigative expenses; prosecution; the courts; legal fees; jury and witness expenses; monies spent on the incarceration, parole, probation, and rehabilitation of offenders; victim services, such as shelters, lawyers, counseling; victim compensation programs; the lost productivity and taxes that injured victims would otherwise be contributing to the greater good; and the wide variety of crime prevention programs and equipment that our fear of crime drives us to seek.

Add the crimes of murder, spouse and child abuse, arson, and vandalism, and it is clear that violence in America today is very expensive. But we pay for such violence not only with money; there are other, often greater expenses. As violent crimes occur and mount in frequency, victims and often their families pay heavily in terms of stress, pain, suffering, and injury, as well as in the reduced quality of life that often follows victimization. The rest of us pay dearly too, especially in our growing fear of crime and in the many freedom-restricting, precautionary steps such fear leads us to take.

Violent crime toward our fellow citizens is very expensive. Its financial and human costs are great. The same is true for violence toward property. Take but one example, school vandalism. As one school principal noted:

> It's hard to say what caused the two boys to do what they did, though both of them had been in trouble with the law outside of school. They broke in one night and just totally vandalized the new wing we just finished in our building. They smashed every inside window and put holes with a BB gun or something in every plate glass window to the outside. They sure must have taken their time, because there's not even one window in the entire wing that wasn't smashed or shot.
>
> Then they broke into the library and knocked over all the shelves. There were hundreds and hundreds of books scattered all over the floor. My office too, administration. They got a set of keys and were able to get where our duplicating machine and switchboard are. I think they are both destroyed beyond repair. Worst of all, they set two fires—one on the first floor and one on the third. The one on the first floor got put out pretty quickly, but they must have lit the one upstairs first, because it totally destroyed three classrooms.
>
> All of this, they said, because their teacher really made them angry.

What must we all pay to undo such wanton destruction? The costs in money include

- The fire and police department's investigation of the act and pursuit of the vandals
- Custodial labor to clean up the debris
- Clerical costs for preparing work orders and ordering building materials
- Operating vehicles to transport workers and materials to the job site
- Materials, labor, and other construction costs
- Transporting students to other schools
- Loss of classroom availability during repairs and construction
- Loss of income from canceled athletic events

With so many direct and hidden impacts, no wonder the most recent estimate of the financial cost of school vandalism in the United States has reached 600 million dollars! Furthermore, just as with rape, robbery, assault, and all other violent crimes against people, violence toward property exacts a high price in human costs. Think of yourself as the child going to the vandalized school or that child's parent. You feel vulnerable, angry, fearful, suspicious. All of which also affects the school's own educational effort.

Who pays? We all do, and we pay a great deal. No wonder there is growing interest in America today in forcefully shifting at least some of this burden back to the perpetrators of such violence in terms of restitution to victims by offenders, partial payment for services received by prison inmates, restorative community service by offenders not incarcerated. Surely, such repayment plans will grow more and more popular in America as the costs of aggression in our society continue to grow.

Is Aggression Always Bad?

aggression in both laboratory and real life is usually defined by researchers as intentional physical or psychological injury to another person or to property. For these same researchers, and for therapists, ministers, politicians, as well as most of the rest of us, aggression is a behavior to be controlled, reduced, or eliminated. It is, I agree, harmful, hurtful, antisocial, and immoral.

A parent hits his child and gets obedience. One neighbor screams insults at another and gets submission. The bully threatens the whipping boy in the school yard and takes his lunch money. A teacher hits a student and gets compliance. A husband beats his wife and feels macho. These are all common examples of aggression, in fact successful aggression from each perpetrator's point of view, that clearly qualify as harmful, hurtful, antisocial, and immoral.

But is aggression always bad? Are there circumstances in which intentional physical or psychological injury is, despite the pain inflicted, appropriate, prosocial, and quite moral? I can think of four possible scenarios in which, perhaps, aggression makes good sense:

■ A toddler, perhaps a year old, has begun walking and is energetically "on the move" and exploring his world. Physically, he is now able to run into the street, walk over to the stove and reach the burners, or otherwise injure himself. Yet he is not cognitively developed enough to have learned that the word no, even spoken harshly, means stop doing whatever you are doing. A painful smack on the butt as the word no is spoken may well arm that word with its needed stopping power.

▪ A young woman is walking down a neighborhood street one evening and two burly adolescent males come up from behind and begin taunting her. One circles in front while the second makes an unsuccessful grab for her purse. In the attempt, her purse is sprung open. She reaches in, grabs a canister of pepper spray, and sprays both youths in the face.

▪ A nervous and agitated man clutching a box on his lap captures the attention of the transit police in one large city's subway system. They stop and question him. He becomes abusive, drops the box, and tries to run away. As one officer restrains him, the second opens the box and finds four sticks of dynamite wired to a timer. The man shouts, "You may have gotten that one, but you'll never find the other two before they go off!" Fearing that many innocent lives may be at stake, the officers twist the man's arms quite painfully to get him to reveal the location of the other bombs.

▪ Grandma has suffered a long time with her illness. Her pains grow worse daily, and she more and more insistently and plaintively asks her son to help end her life, as she is far too debilitated to do so alone. One quiet night in the hospital, they say their goodbyes. He sedates her as best he can with some pills he has hoarded, then puts a plastic bag over her head until she stops breathing.

Teaching safe and unsafe places to a young child, acting in self-defense when assaulted, torturing a perpetrator to save innocent lives, and performing euthanasia: Perhaps none of these are easy calls. Some psychologists (including me) have long said, Never hit a child. Self-defense when assaulted seems defensible, but even here there can be disagreement if the response too greatly exceeds the cause; for example, if the woman had shot and killed rather than sprayed the two street thieves.

Much more contentious, and clearly a matter for continuing ethical, religious, and moral debate, are the use of torture to save innocent lives and euthanasia to take a life in pain. By definition, both may be considered aggression. Their use for these positive ends, as with the smacking of the wandering toddler and the spraying of the assailants, raises the question, Is aggression always bad?

I think about this question a lot. Maybe more of us should.

America the Safe

much of the United States is scared out of its wits. Many of our citizens imagine a criminal lurking in each dark alley, a burglar casing each darkened home, a rapist eying a prospective victim from behind each rustling curtain.

It is no wonder that fear of becoming a crime victim is so great—and so very much greater than actual statistical chances of victimization. Our lives are buried in crime descriptions, crime predictions, and recommended crime precautions.

Most of our television and newspaper news stories describe the unusual event; the usual is usually not worth telling. Several years ago, a rape was committed in a city park near where I work. The day after it happened, a newspaper reporter called me to discuss it. As we talked, he asked what I thought would be the impact of this unfortunate event on the community's use of the park. I responded by estimating that on the same warm, sunny day that the rape occurred, probably five hundred people peacefully enjoyed the same park. Would he report that too, I asked. His answer was that people strolling, playing, or relaxing in a park wasn't news, a rape was.

If our media—for reasons of reader interest, commercial profit, or journalistic custom—report only their usually very heavy diet of murder, rape, assault, fraud, burglary, and other crimes, and find the usual in human behavior not newsworthy, it distorts how we see our world and increases our fears.

Early in my own career, I spent a great deal of time training police officers and repeatedly saw how the typical cop, working all day in his or her community's criminal "underbelly," then relaxing each evening with fellow officers exchanging "war stories," was led to a distorted view of the human condition.

In recent years, one of the main topics of my own work has been school violence and what to do about it. I think about it, read about it, lecture about it, research it, and spend countless hours in high-violence school settings. In order to avoid the crime-is-overwhelming-us distortion, I constantly remind myself that—just like in our papers and on TV—what I see and hear is only a very small slice of the complete story.

Approximately 97 percent of our public school children go to school every day, learn their lessons reasonably well, enjoy being there, and come home safely. From the outcry about the lack of safety in America's public schools, one would never know it. When one of the politicians in my city who unfortunately said he would only visit our local high schools if he were armed, he was engaging in this very form of gross overgeneralizing.

When good stuff happens, it is routine, commonplace, boring, and not newsworthy. In contrast, a crime causes a media feeding frenzy. Story after story after story. Fear levels rise and themselves become news, perpetrating a scare spiral. Crime-precaution feature stories follow. Nail your windows shut, buy this or that superlock, install an alarm system, get a barking dog, learn self-defense, turn your home into a fortress, pressure your politicians to permit the carrying of concealed weapons. Fear drives these behaviors; these behaviors themselves further increase fearfulness. (If I'm actually doing these things, there must really be something to be afraid of!).

Something must break into this fear spiral and bring it into closer touch with actual crime victimization probabilities. Of course one should be prudent, one should not bury one's head in the sand. But let us all try harder to go about our lives based on the realities that face us, not fearful, distorted imaginings. For the most part, we all still live in America the safe.

Odds 'n' Ends
About Aggression

there are a number of additional facts, figures, fictions, and realities about violence in America worth noting here, as they help set the stage for the lessons that follow.

■ Perhaps because of an influx of weapons in the hands of returning soldiers now more comfortable in the use of such arms—and because war makes violence more legitimate and acceptable whether a nation was defeated or victorious—homicide rates tend to increase after a war. In the United States, this growth in postwar murder occurred after the Civil War, both world wars, and the Vietnam war.

■ The more unequal men and women are with power, authority, and decision making primarily in male hands, the greater the level of rape and wife-beatings.

■ Aggression is a remarkably stable behavior. Research consistently shows that the frequently aggressive child or adolescent is very likely to grow up to be a highly aggressive adult, more likely not only to commit violent crimes but also drunk driving, severe punishment of offspring, and spouse abuse. One long-term study showed a significant relationship between the level of violence at eight years of age and antisocial acts twenty-two years later.

■ Some researchers suggest that, contrary to popular opinion, girls are *not* less aggressive than boys but instead that they just express aggression in ways different from the physical acts common for aggressive boys. Examples are interpersonal rejection or shunning; manipulation; gossip; passive aggression, such as refusal or inaction; and related means.

■ Aggression grows not only from forces within the person, such as perceptions, emotions, thoughts, and the like; it is also stimulated by objects and events outside the person. Some research, for example, suggests that not only can a gun be a means for the expression of aggression caused by internal forces but also that the mere presence of a gun can itself stimulate aggression. As the researchers put it, sometimes "the trigger pulls the finger."

■ An interesting but rarely studied form of aggression is booing by an audience. Research shows that unlike applause, which typically occurs immediately after well-liked presentations and which results from independent decisions to do so by individual members of the audience, booing begins after a delay of as long as two seconds following disapproved presentations and typically only after audience members monitor each other's behavior to be sure they are not booing alone.

■ Homicide is the most common cause of death for young African-American females as well as for young African-American males. The probability of a young African-American female dying of homicide is four times that of a non–African-American female. A young African-American male is eleven times more likely to die from homicide than a non–African-American male.

■ Few differences among people of different races are found in their rates of violence when people being compared are at the same income level. What does seem to contribute to the high levels of violent crime by certain ethnic minority groups is their sense of deprivation compared to others, their lack of opportunity to better their life circumstances, the racism and discrimination they frequently experience, and the survival values that grow from these experiences.

■ Estimates are that between 40 percent and 50 percent of American households have guns, and half of them are handguns. Approximately 220 million firearms are in the hands of private citizens in the United States, and perhaps as many as 3 million of these are large-clip, automatic, and semi-automatic assault weapons.

■ Sexual violence in film and on television shows graphic rape, torture, murder, and mutilation scenes, very often with women as victims. Such depictions have been shown to increase the callousness of male viewers toward women, increase their belief that women desire to be raped and deserve sexual abuse, and also increase their actual level of aggressiveness when they interact with women.

■ When dating couples fight, physically, what is it that typically lights the fuse? Studies indicate that for such couples, the major aggression-arousing problems involve jealousy, verbal abuse, interferences of friends, interferences of other activities, lack of time together, and a breakdown of the relationship itself. Also common sources of couples fighting are drug or alcohol use, sexual problems, conflicting plans for the future, and dating someone else.

■ Research on the effects of nutrition on aggressive behavior is just beginning. Some evidence suggests that deficiencies in thiamine and perhaps other vitamins, too little of the minerals of iron or magnesium, and an excess of lead or cadmium in the body can influence levels of aggression. A number of foods and food additives may also be implicated, with some studies pointing to too much intake of milk as a particular cause of aggressive actions.

2.

why?
causes of
violent behavior

Internal Causes

*Characteristics of People
That Make Aggression
More Likely*

Learning to Be Aggressive

It was once thought that we all have an instinct for aggression, a combative energy that must be expressed. For many years, it was recommended to repetitively aggressive people—spouse abusers, child abusers, and others who regularly behaved violently—that they find a safe substitute for this inevitable instinctive energy. Blow off steam. Beat on the couch, or the punching bag, or the bobo doll instead.

In recent years, however, such catharsis thinking about aggression has changed, as the idea of an inborn and inevitable aggressive instinct has been shown to be a convenient but incorrect myth. Instead, a great deal of research has demonstrated that aggression is primarily learned behavior, learned the same way any other behavior is learned, by observation, imitation, direct experience, rehearsal, and the like.

If it is learned, who is teaching it and where? Clearly, a major classroom for the teaching and learning of aggression is the home. For many persons, the process begins with interactions described by the Oregon Social Learning Center as "coercive parenting." This is parental behavior that is frequently irritable and inconsistent. At times, the parents' supervision of the child is overly lax or even nonexistent, at other times harsh and severe. The coercion takes the form of threats, reprimands, and corporal punishment.

There are two consequences: Children stop "misbehaving" (temporarily) often enough that the parents are encouraged to continue being coercive. Second, by imitation, children learn that being coercive themselves can be a good way to get what they want. Temper tantrums, whining, yelling, and hitting are growing techniques for controlling those coercive parents. By age two or three, such children are often called "temperamental."

As ages four, five, and six approach, such youngsters become social beings. They go outside to play with other children. Having learned in the home that coercion pays, that might makes right, they begin employing aggressive tactics with newfound peers. Johnny pushes Mary off her tricycle so that he can have a ride. He grabs Freddie's soccer ball and runs off to kick it around. He barges ahead of three or four other children waiting their turns on the slide. Mary's mom, Freddie's dad, and the parents of the children on line each object, intervene, and tell their children not to play with Johnny because he doesn't play nicely.

Johnny's parents have not served as positive models for him, and now the peers, who in some ways could, are withdrawn for their own protection. Johnny— who might now be labeled an oppositional child—still has social needs, still desires playmates, and begins to gravitate toward and play with other coercive, frequently aggressive children. He enters school already primed for trouble, and it doesn't take him long to find it. Regularly using the aggressive behaviors he has already learned so well, he becomes a "difficult" child, a "problem" child, an "acting-out" child, perhaps receiving the formal label of *conduct disorder*.

Among school personnel and his fellow students, Johnny's reputation often precedes him. He is seen as a likely troublemaker; because he is unskilled at other ways of getting along and because his aggression usually brings attention and approval from his violence-prone friends, he works hard to live up to this negative expectation. If such lessons about the success of aggression continue, the frequency of aggressive acts and their level of intensity grow. By preteen or teen years, "conduct disorder" has given way to "juvenile delinquent."

Johnny has learned his lessons well.

Us Versus Them

groups may compete with each other, blame each other for this or that, grow angry with each other, and even fight and kill one another. Such aggression between groups has always been a main feature of human relations. Tribes; clans; gangs; ethnic, religious, or regional groups; or even whole nations are often in deadly conflict with one another.

The reasons are many, but one very important source is *us versus them* thinking. A basic human quality is the desire to feel one is part of a group of people whom we see as being both like ourselves and special in some important way—such as better than other groups. One researcher described it as the need for allies and enemies.

Us versus them thinking is especially strong when groups compete. The competition may be among teens over the outcome of an athletic event, gangs over who owns a piece of turf, or nations struggling for resources or power. In all cases, the psychological outcome is the same—there is more attachment to one's own group (us) and more hostility toward the other group (them).

A group of British researchers, in their experiments on what they called the *minimal group*, showed the power of us versus them thinking even when the people involved were randomly put into one of two groups by a flip of a coin done in front of them. These were clearly not real groups to which the person had become attached. In fact, no one was even given the opportunity to meet the other members of his or her artificial group. Nevertheless, in a number of ways, people showed clear favoritism to their own group and regular discrimination toward the other group.

Our self-esteem, our sense of security, our own importance seems very much tied to the success of the groups to which we belong. We favor our own groups at the expense of other groups in order to build these positive qualities in ourselves. Unfortunately, "at the expense of" often means much more than friendly competition—and can mean deadly combat.

Is it inevitable that groups must fight? Are there ways of eliminating or at least reducing such aggression, and the suspicion, mistrust, tension, and stereotyping that seem to cause it?

One early view was that conflict between groups was a result of ignorance. Bring us and them together, it was believed, and from such contact they would learn enough about each other that their misinterpreting would decrease and along with it their aggression toward each other. The brotherhood meetings, intergroup summer camps, interracial dinners, and educational campaigns of the 1940s and 1950s were among the several ways such us-them contact was carried out.

Research on these efforts, as well as on interracial housing and employment in the armed forces, showed that contact alone was not enough. For conflict between groups to decrease, there had to be certain types of contact. Contact between groups will decrease hostility if it is cooperative contact, such as when there is a challenging circumstance both wish to resolve but neither can resolve alone. Contact will also be successful when it is frequent, not rare; when it is personal, not casual; and when the meeting of us and them has the support of law, community climate, or another important source.

We fight partly because we are a "we" and they are somebody else. If the us-them gap can be narrowed, if they too can be seen as individuals and not as stereotypes, if they can be seen as like us in significant ways, such conflict between groups can diminish.

Aggressive Thoughts
and Aggressive Actions

thoughts lead to actions. Most people, most of the time, choose not to behave aggressively, because they think such actions are immoral, antisocial, and just plain wrong.

Persons who are frequently angry and aggressive—especially those who commit violent crimes—act differently than most of us. Do they think differently also? The answer from researchers studying the thought processes of violent persons clearly seems to be yes. How do they think? What are their thoughts?

First, their thinking is typically *self-centered.* "When I get mad, I don't care who gets hurt." "If I see something I like, I take it." "If I want to do something, I don't care if it's legal or not." Their view of their world is "me first."

Hand in hand with such an egocentric way of seeing things, persons who are frequently aggressive often *view others as being hostile* toward them even when they are not. They misinterpret neutral behavior by others, seeing it, instead, as aggression directed toward them. This is why so many youths interpret being looked at (a neutral act) as a challenge, threat, or put-down (a hostile act). Similarly, if they are accidentally bumped in a crowded school hallway between classes, they believe it is intentional.

Self-centered thinking and seeing hostility from others even when it is not there, in the thinking of people who are frequently aggressive, call for a response. The first response is often a *mislabeling* of what must be done, such as "I have to defend myself," or "Hitting him will knock some sense into him," or "No way I can let him get away with it."

Mislabeling often combines with two other common thinking distortions to make aggression almost inevitable. One is called *assuming the worst* ("If I don't smack him I'll look like a punk"). The other is called *externalizing* or *blaming others* ("It's his fault, he's asking for it, I'll smack him").

Added to this are two more distorted ways of thinking about the world, and again both make aggression more likely. One is called *false consensus:* the rationalization that other people think and act as I do, nothing unusual about me. *Anchoring,* the final thinking mode common in aggressors, is a resistance to changing one's thinking, even when new evidence to the opposite comes along.

So there you have it: self-centeredness, seeing hostility not there, mislabeling, assuming the worst, blaming others, false consensus, and anchoring. These are the thinking distortions commonly made by chronically aggressive children, adolescents, and adults.

Thoughts *do* lead to actions. It is clear then that in trying to reduce aggressive behavior in our society, a good first step is to work on changing the kinds of thinking likely to lead to such behavior.

Aggression as Addiction

aggression, at least for some individuals, behavior to which they are addicted? I have not seen aggression described this way by others, and certainly the term *addiction* is much overused by society today. But it is nevertheless curious that aggressive behavior often has so much in common with addiction to drugs, alcohol, tobacco, gambling, and other habit-forming substances and activities. Just as is true for each of these several "traditional" addictions, for some individuals aggression is

■ A long-term, repetitively used, unusually stable behavior. The chronically aggressive youngster is exceedingly likely to become a chronically aggressive adult.

■ A behavior that provides short-term satisfaction but long-term problems. Beyond mere "satisfaction" or pleasure, some youths even describe an addiction-like, physical "rush" accompanying their violent acts.

■ Frequently accompanied by denial: "I didn't do it" or "I didn't mean it" or "I didn't start it." Such denial, minimizing, and attribution of responsibility to others is the smoker's song, the drug addict's rejoinder, the aggressor's frequent response.

■ Described as behavior that is difficult to control, very hard to reduce, and at times feels like a compulsion. When some time passes without aggression, there are likely to be frequent relapses and a return to aggressive actions.

■ Used for a variety of reasons, including to relieve stress, deal with unpleasantness from others, alter a negative mood, and reduce a heightened level of physical arousal.

■ Sustained not only by its quality of "feeling good" but also by the encouragement and support of others, many of whom could be described as friend and family "enablers." Such encouragement is also often provided by mass media portrayals and community tradition. Drink beer, bet on the lottery, light up a smoke, don't take lip from anybody—all common American themes.

■ A preoccupation they have with the use of the behavior by other people, be it drug taking, gambling, or aggression. Chronic aggressors, for example, watch much more television violence than do others less prone to such behavior.

■ A behavior that results in a high level of health risk, risk of injury, and even death.

If it does prove to make sense to consider aggression as addictive behavior, then what is known about the causes of other addictions, and their cure, may some day aid us in better understanding what motivates the chronically violent individual and how we may best prevent or reduce such damaging behavior.

How to Hurt Someone
and Not Feel Guilty

when a grievance, frustration, or anger makes me feel like punching you in the face, and yet I am held back by my civility, my upbringing, and my feelings of guilt as I imagine doing it, what may go on in my own head to tip the balance and permit me to punch away? More generally, how can people behave aggressively toward others, even cruelly, without condemning themselves for doing so? According to Professor Albert Bandura at Stanford University, several self-deceptive, rationalizing processes may take place.

■ **Minimization of one's own aggression by comparing it with worse behavior by others.** "OK, I punched him and kicked him in the head, but at least I used my own fists and feet, not a knife or gun like some guys do."

■ **Justification of one's own aggression in terms of higher moral principles.** Perhaps the best example of this type of self-vindication and denial of responsibility is the frequent recourse taken by nations at war to the claim that "God is on our side" and the companion notion that theirs is a righteous, holy battle.

■ **Displacement of responsibility.** Here the individual avoids ownership of his or her own aggressive behavior by shifting responsibility for it to a higher authority, an authority willing to assume such responsibility. The commonly heard plea by those on trial for war crimes that they "were just following orders" is a prime illustration of such displacement to higher ranking others.

■ **Diffusion of responsibility**. Aggression, especially on a large scale, may require for its enactment the services of many different people, each contributing their small part to the larger effort. It is often possible under such circumstances to make each contribution seem and feel relatively harmless, especially if the persons involved are kept (by others or themselves) relatively ignorant of the overall aggressive effort. The Nazi concentration camp death machine, a product composed of many individual contributions, well illustrates such diffusion of responsibility.

■ **Dehumanization of victims.** It appears to be the case that the greater the empathy we feel for another person, the more we perceive his or her world and humanness, the less able we are to hurt him or her. The opposite also apparently is true. The more we are able to view someone as something less than human, or even as of another species, the more readily aggression toward that person is possible. Racial or religious stereotyping, the view of the enemy in wartime, or even our attitude toward fans of the other team at a heated sports contest are each good examples of our tendency to give such persons a demeaning label or name, see the others as "them" and unlike "us," and via such dehumanizing enable ourselves to hurt them.

■ **Deindividuation.** This is a guilt-reducing, aggression-promoting phenomenon that often occurs in riots, mob or crowd violence, or other forms of group aggression. Each person, in a sense, temporarily loses his or her individual identity to become part of a larger collective. Rather than a spreading out, sharing, or diffusion of responsibility as we have described, deindividuation instead serves as a denial of responsibility. The highly emotional, aggressive collective violence by large groups of fans at soccer, football, or other athletic matches illustrates this quality well.

■ **Attribution of blame to victims.** A related but different type of denial of responsibility for one's own aggressive behavior is to hold its target responsible. As Professor Bandura put it, here "aggressors see themselves as essentially persons of good will who are forced into punitive actions by villainous opponents." Victims, it is held, bring it on themselves. Not uncommonly, youths who are chronically delinquent or adults who are career criminals are adept at trying to explain away their antisocial behavior with detailed descriptions of how the victims' stupidity, resistance, hesitancy, or other qualities "made me do it."

■ **Graduated desensitization.** Repeated performance of unpleasant behavior, especially when taken in small steps, can progressively decrease its unpleasantness and increase its perpetrator's tolerance for and acceptance of both the behavior itself and his or her own self-perception as an individual capable of doing such things. In this manner, the level of aggression can gradually increase, until eventually the perpetrator can carry out cruel and violent acts with little discomfort. A good illustration of such graduated desensitization is our description of the manner in which torturers are trained (see page 142).

■ **Hygienic positioning.** Here the aggressor positions himself or herself at sufficient distance from the impact or consequences of his or her own violent behavior in order to deny it. Sometimes this distancing is literally true, as when a soldier fires a missile or large artillery piece to a distant target or a bombardier drops bombs from an altitude of many miles. Other times, the distancing is figurative, such as when verbal deniers are used to describe one's own aggressive acts; for example, the victim was "offed" or "wasted," not "killed" or "murdered," or, as in concentration camp terminology, "units were processed" rather than "human beings were slaughtered."

When you stop and think about it, as we seldom do, our ability to avoid taking responsibility for our own aggression is both quite remarkable and quite dismaying.

Low Empathy, High Aggression

empathy is the ability to take others' perspectives, to see things through their eyes, feel what they feel, walk in their shoes. In important ways, empathy and aggression are opposites. The more you have of one of these qualities, the less you are likely to have the other.

To make someone behave aggressively, minimize empathy for the intended victim. In the military forces of all countries, combat training places great emphasis on dehumanizing the enemy, on minimizing empathy: See how tall (short), fat (skinny) they are. Look at the color of their skin, the shape of their eyes, the way they talk. They don't eat regular food like us, they eat dog (or eel, or whatever). They're not people, they are _____." (The negative label varies from country to country and from one war to another.)

At all levels of human groups—tribes, crowds, gangs, mobs, regions, nations—such us versus them thinking lowers empathy and makes aggression more possible. We can easily see the world of, feel the feelings of, stand in the shoes of fellow members of our "us" group but often have great difficulty doing so for "them."

How can "they" be made to seem more like "real people" and in a sense more like "us"? How can a Crip gang member be encouraged to empathize with a Blood gang youth? A biased White with an African American? An abusive husband with his abused wife? A gay-basher with a gay person? The answers are not easy, because we often work so hard to keep our biases, our distance from and angry fictions about other people.

Some aggressors seem not just weak in empathy but lacking in it altogether. Last year, two youngsters, ages ten and eleven, held a five-year-old child by his feet out a fourteenth story window because he had refused to steal candy for them. Then they dropped him. Try to look beyond the horror of this murder, to see inside the heads of the two perpetrators. What, in their minds, were they holding? What did the dropping mean? To them, was this boy an inanimate object, a member of another species?

Such low-empathy youngsters are rare, but they do damage well beyond their numbers. Many used to be labeled *psychopaths*. Now the U.S. Department of Justice calls them Serious Habitual Offenders, the "SHO kids." They are the 7 percent of juvenile delinquents who commit over 50 percent of all felonies by juveniles. They are the over and over again recidivists, committing crime after crime, often accompanied by serious violence. When caught, they show no remorse for their victim, no guilt.

Trying such adolescents as adults and incarcerating them for long prison sentences has so far been America's primary response to their predations. But these youths are America's children also, and so we must ask how they got that way, how a human can grow up with so little empathy for others of the species.

Research has shown that we can place much of the blame on parenting that never happened, or happened too inconsistently, harshly, or even abusively. Studies have clearly shown that abusive parents are chronically deficient in taking their children's perspective and that abused youngsters often grow up to be as empathy deficient as their parents. For some children, the lessons they learn early in life are lessons about pain and punishment from other human beings, and thus their bonding to their own species largely fails to take place. They suffer from what psychologists have called *an attachment disorder*.

Deficiencies in empathy begin at home; so too must the cure.

External Causes

*Characteristics of the Environment
That Make Aggression More Likely*

Television as Tutor:
Aggression 101

you have probably read the litany of numbers somewhere by now: 99 percent of American homes have a television set, and two-thirds have two or more. The average American adolescent watches television approximately thirty-five hours per week. There are an average of six violent acts per hour on prime time evening programming and twenty-five such acts per hour on Saturday morning cartoons. By age sixteen, two hundred thousand violent acts have been seen, about thirty-three thousand of them murders or attempted murders.

Psychologists and other researchers studying human behavior almost always qualify their results when reporting them—"it seems to be," "it probably is true that," "it is likely the case that." No such hedging of bets is necessary here. Many dozens of studies have shown this heavy diet of violence viewing to have three serious and often long-lasting effects.

The first may be called the _copycat effect._ A substantial minority of the viewers will actually do what they have seen. Males copy more than do females, younger children more than older. There is more copying the more violence the youngster has seen, when the violence depicted is justified by the show's script (for example, when the "good guy" wins), when it "works," when it is shown in how-to detail, and when it has that odd quality of painlessness so often depicted—no suffering, no injury, no bodily consequences. Violently erotic shows lead to the most copying; cartoons, sports, and soap operas next; followed by adventure, detective, and crime stories; with news and public affairs shows resulting in the least copying.

The second, well-demonstrated consequence has been called the *victim effect*. Increased fearfulness, mistrust, and self-protectiveness are its main features. We come to see the world differently, as more threatening, less safe. Millions of (especially elderly) American citizens sentence themselves to solitary confinement every night, fearful of becoming a crime victim to an extent that is out of proportion to its actuarial likelihood. This fearfulness is, in part, an effect of television.

The final consequence, and perhaps the most serious, is the *desensitization effect*. As the violence levels depicted increase in intensity and graphic detail, we adapt, we adjust, we get used to it. Current fare includes spurting arteries, chainsaw dismemberment, violent rape scenes. We adapt, we adjust, we get used to it. Such desensitization and increased callousness present a major problem for the revenue-driven television industry, because, as we adapt to a level of violence, it becomes less stimulating, less interesting, and thus less desirable to watch. If we don't watch the program, we don't watch the commercial. Thus, to command our attention, producers must program ever-higher levels of violence. It is difficult to imagine what may be shown next: a type of "hemovision" in which blood spurts from the set onto your living room rug? Or the "snuff film," in which the actors are actually killed?

Thus far, corrective steps either contemplated or enacted at the industry or even at congressional levels have been ineffective, concentrating primarily on one or another type of rating system. Very little energy has been directed to encouraging or creating significant amounts of interesting nonviolent programming.

Our children go to two schools every day, often for five hours each. One is a building with teachers, classrooms, books, chalk, and erasers. The other is a box with a large picture tube, dials, cables, and the demonstrated ability to have a tremendous influence on the behavior of America's children. Thus far, most of that influence has been for the worse. The potential exists to make television an influence for the common good. As adults, as parents, as citizens, we owe our children no less.

Death by Imitation

series of studies conducted by Professor David Phillips of the University of California and others stimulated by his work strongly shows us the awesome power of our mass media to influence our behavior. It not only substantially shapes how we think, what we feel, how we spend our time and incomes, but also how we die.

In 1974, Phillips reported findings that showed that following newspaper reports of suicides, the frequency of suicides and motor vehicle deaths increased. The greater the publicity, the greater the increase. The increase occurred mainly in the geographic area where the suicide story was published. This seemed to indicate that newspaper suicide stories triggered imitative suicides, some of which were disguised as auto accidents.

A few years later, in a second study, he was able to show the same copycat behavior—but induced by fictional, not real, suicides. Tracking suicides portrayed in television soap operas, he again discovered a significant increase in real-life suicides after the TV shows. The rate was higher for females than males, and the imitative suicides—paralleling the earlier 1974 study—peaked on the third day after the soap opera suicide was shown. The imitation effect also was shown in this research by the significant increase after the fictional suicides in serious but nonfatal single driver automobile accidents, which in this context should be viewed as failed suicide attempts.

Other research has further confirmed such powerful media triggering of life-taking behavior. Two studies again showed the imitative suicide result but only when the person whose suicide was publicized was a celebrity—an entertainment star or a national or international political figure. Again, the greater the publicity, the greater the impact.

Other types of violence can also be prompted by mass media portrayals. One study demonstrated that homicides in the United States increase sharply immediately following heavyweight championship prize fights. As in the suicide studies, homicidal imitative violence peaks the third day after the event. Once again, the greater the publicity, the greater the imitative result. When the losing fighter was White, there was a significant increase in White but not Black homicide victims. When the losing fighter was Black, there was a significant increase in Black but not White homicide victims, results again readily explained by mass media–induced imitation.

Homicides may also be primed by media portrayals of other violent reports and again have special triggering implications for the losers. One researcher tested this idea on professional football games. His prediction was that homicide rates would increase significantly after such contests, particularly in the cities of the losing teams. Probably as a result of both imitation of the media-portrayed violent behavior and frustration over losing, the results were exactly as predicted. Thus, on December 24, 1977, Denver beat Baltimore, and in the week that followed, the homicide rate increased substantially in Baltimore but not in Denver, with similar results for more than fifty other such playoff games in the cities with losing teams.

Clearly, violence in the mass media—real or fictional, life-taking or merely severe—can be and is imitated.

Interestingly, the mass media not only helps cause violent behavior in its viewers and readers, its popularity also serves as an accurate index of the violence level of a particular area or region. One investigator studied the circulation rates of forty-eight magazines across the fifty states. Three types of magazines were involved, which he called *urbane cultivated interests* (for example, *Business Week, House and Garden, New Yorker*); *mainstream* (for example, *Reader's Digest, Good Housekeeping, McCalls*); and, of interest to us here, *machismo* (such as *Shooting Times, Playboy,* and *Muscle and Fitness*).

States highest in machismo-type magazine circulation were (in order) Alaska, Nevada, Hawaii, Wyoming, New Mexico, Colorado, and Arizona. Interestingly, these are primarily the most recent states to achieve statehood. The frontier still lives! Independent surveys show, in these states in particular, high levels of opposition to gun control as well as strong support for increased military spending, the death penalty, and the use of force under a variety of circumstances. Beliefs as well as behavior are machismo in these states. Compared to states with lower machismo scores based on magazine circulation, the seven high-machismo states have well above average rates of burglary, larceny, rape, accidental death, suicide, and homicide.

Mass media, then, can teach our citizens violence by imitation as well as teach us about our citizens and their behavior. The old saying was, "You are what you eat." Perhaps, with regard to violence, it would be more accurate to say, "You are what you read."

Alcohol and Aggression: Courage in a Bottle

the connection is absolutely clear: Alcohol and aggression are very close companions. Many separate studies in several countries over a period of many years consistently show high levels of alcohol consumption in a large percentage of perpetrators of homicide, rape, assault, and robbery. For homicide and rape, a substantial number of victims are also either drunk or under the influence.

Making the same connection, other researchers have shown the violent crime rate in particular areas to rise or fall as the availability of liquor increased (new liquor stores in previously dry areas; a lowering of the legal drinking age; counties permitting sale of alcoholic beverages by-the-drink for the first time) or decreased (closing of liquor stores due to an employee strike; rationing; significant price increases).

That drinking and violence are frequently associated there can be no doubt. The interesting question is, What are the processes that cause this connection to happen? Research on human perception, thinking, and behavior has provided some good answers. Such research has shown that when a person drinks an excessive amount of alcohol, a series of changes happen that logically promote the likelihood of aggression. First, there is what psychologists call a narrowing of the perceptual field. The person pays attention to fewer things in the immediate environment and is thus less aware of what is going on around him or her.

Since future time perspective also decreases and attention becomes focussed almost exclusively on the present, the person registers and responds much more to the immediate situation—with diminished concern for longer-term consequences.

The ability to think abstractly and to verbalize decline when one is under the influence of alcohol. Both of these deficiencies decrease the chances that, if a conflict emerges, the person will be able to find peaceable means for resolving it.

In addition to the here-and-now focus and the decreased ability to bring in and use alternative solutions, the probability of violence is increased by the manner in which drinking enhances the drinker's sense of power and mastery. As one researcher put it, a man of power has certain rights and privileges. Events and irritations that others may ignore may require aggressive response from the powerful. For many, there is indeed courage in the bottle.

Aggression, as is true of all human behavior, grows not only from qualities within but also from the physical and social setting in which the person operates. Bars are a frequent location of violence not only because of the effects of alcohol but also because the bars themselves are considered in our society to be "time-out" places in which antisocial behavior can be at least partially blamed on the bottle.

Bars are also places for self-image promotion. Based on her interviews of two hundred bartenders, one researcher reported that refusal to serve a patron was the single most frequent reason for an aggressive dispute to begin, a finding likely related to an "I can hold my liquor" image promotion.

Bars are not only sites for aggression between patrons or patron and bartender. Bars are also magnets, as it were, for aggression on the blocks and in the neighborhoods in which they are located. They do, after all, attract people who are vulnerable (or will be, after drinking), have cash on hand, and thus are suitable crime targets. Within such a setting, or around it, alcohol is a powerful primer of forces that lead to violence. Some do the drinking, but many pay the price.

Perhaps, then, we would be wise to build on the fact noted earlier that as alcoholic beverages become less available, violent crime decreases. I would recommend higher prices; higher taxes; restrictions on advertising; changes in the permitted density of bars, taverns, and other drinking outlets; and regulations limiting the days and hours of operation for drinking establishments and retail liquor stores. Though Prohibition failed and hardly anyone anymore remembers the anti-drinking activist groups of that era, to a large extent their message was on the right track.

Does the Victim
Help Cause the Violence?

every act of aggression—whether it is child or spouse abuse, a street mugging, rape, or murder—involves at least two people. We usually call one the *perpetrator*, the other the *victim*. But is there a clear line between them? Does the victim, not only the perpetrator, contribute to the violence?

Children who are abused often differ both physically and behaviorly from children who are not abused. Even within the same family, when abuse happens, not all the children are equally likely to be its target. Premature youngsters, those with physical handicaps, those who are ill or otherwise fragile, those who are irritable, fussy eaters, withdrawn, overly demanding, or who fail to respond to parent hugs or other acts of affection are more likely to be abused.

Parent frustration, anxiety, disappointment, or depression in response to such challenging child-raising tasks may help explain, but certainly not excuse, the parent's abusiveness. In a sense, we may say that qualities of the child contributed to the child's victimization, but the child is blameless. The victim here definitely did not cause the violence.

Sometimes the victim clearly does share the blame. Research on what has been called victim-precipitated murder describes a type of homicide in which one person threatens and insults the other, perhaps flashes a weapon, and begins assaulting the other. The second person responds by killing the first. To the police, the murderer here is the perpetrator, but to us, so too is the victim.

It is interesting to note that a large percentage of victim-precipitated murders involve husbands killed by their wives, and these are murders in which the victim (but not the offender) was intoxicated.

Unlike what we have just described, blameless murder victims have qualities that may also contribute to their victimization. Many of these qualities influence how threatened the perpetrator feels and thus how likely he is to pull the trigger. Some of these qualities are the age and apparent physical condition of the victim, that is, his or her potential for retaliating, the victim's passivity or resistance, and how many people the perpetrator is facing at one time.

What about rape? Here, the unfortunate tendency to blame the victim still persists far too often. She "brought it on" or "provoked" the rape by her appearance (clothing, makeup) or her behavior (she asked him out, she let him pay for the date, she had a drink with him). Divorced women victims are more likely to be blamed (by males, not females) than are married women, as are women who knew the perpetrator before the rape, were friends or had dated the rapist.

Some of our society's myths support the idea that much of the blame belongs to the rape victim: Women cannot be raped against their will; women secretly wish to be raped; most accusations of rape are false. There is no basis in fact for any of these beliefs, yet they persist, and victims are victimized a second time by being held partly or fully responsible for their victimization.

Sadly, hospital staff, police, courts, the press, and the victim's husband or boyfriend may also blame her for her own rape often enough that she, like many such victims, may come to blame herself too.

Certainly, every act of aggression involves at least two people. In some instances, one of them is the perpetrator and the other the victim, and which is which is totally clear. In many other instances, the victim provokes the aggression. Perpetrator and victim in reality often share responsibility for the aggression.

In other cases, such as rape, the victim contributes little or nothing to being attacked but receives blame for most or all of what took place.

While sorting out who does what to whom is a vital step in better understanding and dealing with aggressive events, we must do so in a way that doesn't falsely accuse and thus re-victimize those already hurt.

Hot Days,
Hot Tempers

When summer draws near, each year, should we be worried? Since ancient times, people have believed that temperature influences aggression, that hot days lead to hot tempers. This belief in the connection between heat and anger is reflected in our language about aggression (hot under the collar, boiling with rage, anger flaring up) and aggression reduction (cool off, chill out, ice it). Is this connection merely a myth or is it reality?

Actually, several natural qualities of our environment have long been believed to influence how we feel and what we do or don't do—including aggression. The phase of the moon (full moons especially), barometric pressure, noise, air pollution, and temperature are several examples.

However, though many people believe that each of these are indeed powerful influences on our behavior, including aggressive behavior, it is only temperature that has been shown by research to actually have this impact. Hot temperatures do indeed increase aggression.

The summertime peaking of aggressive criminal behavior was observed and written about often enough in early European countries that by 1833 one writer termed the association the *thermic law of delinquency*.

For murder, assault, rape, and wife battering—but not for nonviolent crimes—comparing hot and cool days, weeks, months, or years in many different parts of the world repeatedly shows the same result: Hot periods yield more violence. So do hot places. For many decades, Southern (warmer) regions and cities in the United States have averaged substantially higher violent crime rates than have Northern locations.

Some researchers wondered if the common result of peak violence in June, July, and August might better be explained not by high temperatures themselves but by the fact that during the summer people are out more, get together in large groups more frequently, perhaps drink more beer to cool off, have more free time. However, the temperature-aggression connection appears even when these alternative explanations are ruled out.

In fact, the connection is so clear that charting violent crimes month by month, as the temperature slowly rises to summer and then falls gradually to winter, shows the rate of aggressive crimes to march right along with it. Such crimes are relatively infrequent in January and February, begin to climb in March and April, peak in May through August (the most violent month), start declining in September and October, and, as one researcher put it, "collapse" in November and December.

One researcher looked for and found the temper-temperature relationship in an unusual place. He studied four professional baseball seasons and in each one showed a strong association between the temperature at the game and the number of batters hit by pitched balls during each game!

How can the temperature-aggression connection best be explained? Why is it so strong that not only are individual violent acts influenced by temperature but also political riots, prison riots, and other forms of group aggression? Both research and common sense provide some reasonable answers. It has been shown (and we can all agree) that when people are hot or quite warm they are more likely to be uncomfortable, irritable, in a bad mood. They are less sociable, think more aggressive thoughts, have a shorter fuse, and, as research shows, are therefore more likely to strike out at others.

When summer again draws near, should we be worried?

Auto Aggression

by its use, its abuse, its advertising image, and many of its names (Charger, Gladiator, Ram, Firehawk, Impulse, Blazer, Samurai, Trooper, Cutlass, Bronco, Tracer, Storm, Probe, Stealth), the automobile is not only a vehicle for transportation, but too often also a vehicle for aggression. Studies of driver behavior over the past forty years not only show that aggressive road behavior has been with us a long time but also that it is growing worse.

In the 1960s and 1970s, driver aggression took form mostly in rude gestures, the desire to injure another driver, excessive use of the horn, and racing other drivers. The surveys of the 1980s showed an escalation to tailgating, deliberate blinding by high headlight beams, deliberate prevention of passing or changing lanes, the throwing of an object, and the showing of a weapon. In the 1990s, auto aggression has reached new levels of intensity: roadway shootings, sniper attacks, carjacking, "bump and rob" crimes, drive-by shootings, suicide and murder crashes.

Who are the aggressive drivers? They tend to be persons who are competitive, irritable, distractible, impulsive, extroverted, and male. But auto aggression, as with all sites for aggression, springs not only from the heart and fist of its perpetrators. The setting, the circumstances, the situation also contribute in important ways.

One research team created a frustrating circumstance for drivers by arranging to have a car, which was stopped at a traffic light, fail to move when the light changed. Some of the time, the stopped vehicle was an expensive one, a new black Chrysler Imperial. Other times it was a rusty old Ford station wagon or a decrepit Rambler. Backed-up drivers honked their horns more, and more quickly, when stuck behind either of the older cars than behind the Chrysler. Male drivers honked more, and more quickly, than female drivers, especially when the driver of the stopped car was a female. Aggression is always at least a two-person affair. Thus in the auto, too, the qualities of the aggressive driver count, but so do the surrounding circumstances: who the other driver is, the type of car, and other qualities.

A growing minority of drivers are carrying guns in their cars. A recent study of drivers required to attend traffic school revealed that 44 percent of them had been charged at by another driver, 36 percent had an object thrown at them while they were driving, 13 percent had been bumped or rammed, 8 percent had a physical fight with another driver, 4 percent had been threatened by a gun, and 5 of the 412 drivers surveyed had actually been shot at while driving.

What goes on while driving that promotes aggression? Raymond Novaco, professor at the University of California, Irvine, is the leading researcher of auto aggression. He suggests four processes that encourage aggression. The first is anger arousal. Chronic exposure to traffic congestion, long commutes, and many of the other stressful features of routine driving are associated with lowered tolerance for frustration, increased blood pressure, and increasingly negative mood. Aggression also stems from the difficulty of the trip. The longer the trip; the greater the number of roads and interchanges traveled; the heavier the traffic; the greater the delays and obstacles to moving ahead, getting home, or getting to the office—the worse the mood.

The third process concerns the anonymity of the driving situation. The typical driver is anonymous, can usually easily leave the scene of aggression and remain unidentified, and can avoid accountability for his or her behavior if desired. Such ability to fade into the shadows makes auto aggression more likely.

Finally, the researchers point to scripts. These are the routine ways that people interpret what they see going on around them. Such scripts help determine how people respond. As the United States continues to become a more aggressive nation, and as the roadway is increasingly seen as a major playing field for aggression, driver scripts increasingly promote violent behavior.

Some good advice: If you are out driving and find yourself about to become involved in an auto aggression confrontation—either as perpetrator or victim—stay in the car, take a deep breath, count from ten to one, think of that nice balmy day you spent at the lake last summer, imagine that you are already home or wherever you are heading. Then, drive on.

Words That Incite

Things People Say Can Hurt a Lot

Words That Hurt

In thinking about aggression, and trying to do something about it, we usually focus on physical acts: punching, kicking, other assaults, muggings, homicide. More often, though, aggression lies in what people say to each other. Words can and do hurt.

Sometimes we speak to hurt; other times our goal is to push the person into changing his or her behavior in some way. Parents and their children, husbands and wives, bosses and employees, teachers and students, rival politicians are all sometime users of verbal aggression.

Verbal aggression may take several forms:

Threats. "If you ask me one more time, I'm going to smack you!"

Swearing. *@!!#%&*

Ridicule. "If you go out looking like that, they'll laugh at you!"

Character attack. "How could you be so dumb?"

Background attack. "You're just like your mother, whine, whine, whine."

Physical appearance attacks. "You always look like such a slob."

Future prediction attacks. "You'll never amount to anything."

Slurs based upon the target's personal characteristics, such as race, religion, gender, sexual orientation.

A recent survey of 3,346 American parents with children under eighteen years of age living at home found that 63 percent of them report one or more instances of swearing, insulting, or other verbal aggression toward their children, averaging thirteen times each year.

Verbal aggression certainly is common, but its consequences should not be taken lightly. What are its effects on the victim? Especially when the person is a chronic target of words that hurt, the result may be shame, guilt, and a major loss of self-esteem. People who are treated like a punching bag feel like a punching bag—beaten down, vulnerable, looking for the next punch. Children who are the frequent target of verbal aggression show more physical aggression, delinquency, and problems with their peers as they grow older, compared to youngsters not subjected to such verbal abuse.

Words that hurt are bad—and not only for the victim. It has been shown many times that the most common response to verbal attack is to attack back. The browbeaten employee, the ridiculed child, the threatened spouse each become more likely to use aggression themselves. Thus, as too many of us know by experience, an escalating spiral may develop in which angry words grow into physical attack.

Words, indeed, can hurt. Watch what you say.

Read This Column, Damn It!

america seems to have become a good bit more foul-mouthed in recent decades. Cursing fills our observations, conversations, and evaluations. Some experts believe it is much more frequent in our large cities, where stress levels, anonymity, and high levels of tolerance combine to let the words flow with only infrequent repercussions. In both real life and fiction, cursing abounds, and not just by men but women and children too.

Cursing by children has grown to be so frequent that it is now recognized as an especially serious problem in not only our secondary schools but our elementary schools also. Students curse each other, their work, their teachers, and often seem to use it as an adjective preceding anything and everything—and they are doing so at younger and younger ages. I have had at least a dozen experienced kindergarten teachers describe this as a brand new experience in their careers, often claiming that many of the cursing young children have absolutely no idea what the words mean!

When children do curse in class, it is often contagious, frequently disruptive, and many times a message to all within earshot that the verbal aggression is about to be followed by physical attack. Why do children swear? A group of researchers at the University of Texas suggest several reasons. Like much else that children do, cursing is a way to get attention—actually a very effective way. Its shock value may draw all kinds of responses from parents, teachers, and other adults, especially alarm, anger, and the need to "stamp it out." Some youngsters may let the curse words fly as an act of rebellion; or in emulation of other children, adolescents, or adults; or because it sounds tough or macho, especially to their peers; or even as part of their growing knowledge of and fascination with bodily organs and sexual acts.

Whatever its purposes, it almost always must be dealt with when it happens. Ignoring it in the hope that lack of attention will make it decrease is usually a bad idea because, unfortunately, even though the teacher may be able to do so, it is typically the case that fellow classmates will not and instead will reward the cursing youth with generous doses of attention. So, if ignoring it rarely works, what else might a teacher (or parent or other adult) try? Reprimands and even spanking are frequently used, but both of these approaches can be objected to for several reasons, and even if they do reduce the amount of cursing, the success will most likely be only temporary and short term. Besides, better methods exist and have been shown to work.

One of them is to reward with praise, approval, or something tangible if the child refrains from cursing in a situation in which he or she normally does, or if the youngster curses less often, less intensely, or more briefly. Negative practice seems to be an effective approach as well. Also called *instructed repetition*, it is a method in which the youngster is encouraged to say the curse word repeatedly until it becomes nonrewarding or even unpleasant to continue. For some children, engaging in such a "swear-down" may even make the word seem funny or silly. A companion means to negative practice is to urge the child to make up nonsense words to use in place of the swear words.

If punishment is your preferred approach, it will work best if used together with the reward-for-improvement and negative practice methods just described. The most effective punishing techniques, especially for lasting results, are the nonviolent means: time out and response cost. Time out is removing the child from the opportunity to receive further teacher or peer attention (or other rewards) following the cursing incident. Time out is not putting the child in a dark or scary place, banishing the child for hours, or shaming or humiliating the child. Instead, it is a few minutes, perhaps ten at most, in quiet, boring isolation.

In response cost, rather than removing the child from potential rewards, as in time out, the rewards are removed from the child. Children who curse must pay the cost. That is, in this method there is a withholding or removal of privileges, tangible rewards, or other reinforcers following any undesirable behavior—in this instance, cursing.

These thoughts about the sources and reduction of cursing are offered in the hope that they will be informative to all readers and especially helpful to those struggling to deal with this common and challenging behavior.

Teasing Isn't Pleasing

although in the hindsight of adulthood it may seem that the teasing often directed toward adolescents and younger children by their peers is merely harmless kidding, ask the adolescents and children themselves. For them, teasing can be painful, even traumatizing aggression directed toward them. Here I look at what teasing is, what causes it, and what are its consequences. True, in the grand scheme of things, it is not the most damaging type of aggression. But it can lead to serious enough effects on the target person that better understanding it and controlling it is important.

Teasing contains three qualities: aggression, humor, and ambiguity about its own seriousness. It may mask criticism and insult and thus actually be aggressive; or it may be gentle and friendly and thus contain little aggression. Research shows that in its most common form it is making fun of someone or something. Sarcasm, tricking the target person into believing something, exaggerated imitation, pointing, making faces, physically pestering, taking something such as the target's hat and refusing to give it back—these are among the several forms that teasing can take.

What are children and adolescents teased about? Mostly their physical appearance, especially being overweight, but also their intellectual performance (either being too slow or too smart), physical and athletic performance, family members, interest in the opposite or same sex, personal hygiene, race, fearfulness, promiscuity, psychological problems, handicapping conditions, and more. The list is long; a youngster seeking to tease another indeed has many choices.

When asked, young people say they tease others because someone teased them first, as a joke, because they disliked the other person, because they were in a bad mood, or because the rest of their group was teasing someone. Much teasing also seems to be motivated by an effort to rein in any behaviors that are too different from the group norm. Thus, not only are unpopular, obese, or intellectually slow children teased a lot but so are those who are popular, good-looking, and intellectually advanced.

Teasing may be an effort to communicate aggression in a safe way, as happens when two youths engage in verbal dueling. It may also, in its more benign expressions, communicate affection and do so in a way that is less embarrassing to the youth than its direct expression would be.

The person being teased has to decode the message, to figure out how much is humor and how much is aggression, as well as just exactly what the teaser was intending to say. Their relationship, the teaser's tone of voice and facial expression, and what was going on just before the tease all go into this decoding effort.

When asked how being teased makes them feel, 97 percent of the elementary school students in one recent survey said angry, embarrassed, hurt, or sad. The teaser may be creating what he or she thinks is harmless fun, but for the target person it is anything but fun. Ten percent respond by fighting, 40 percent by teasing back, 25 percent by trying to ignore it, and only 12 percent say they usually laugh along with the teaser.

Words can and do hurt. Teasing, especially teasing with a bite to it, is not playful behavior to be ignored. It is aggression, to be actively discouraged.

Jump! Jump!
The Suicide-Baiting Crowd

harris Brown was very depressed. His marriage had slowly been going sour for many months, and he had begun to suspect that his wife had a lover. Today at work he had been given a first-hand lesson in the meaning of the word *downsizing*. Twenty-two years at the company, twenty-two faithful, hard-working years. And now a note: not needed anymore, goodbye, clean out your desk by Friday.

He crossed the street to the office building he had looked at from his office for years but never been in. Took the elevator to the twelfth floor. Entered the men's room, opened the window, and crawled out on the ledge.

Harris stood there, gazing down but not really seeing. Looked across the street to his own office, thought about the memo. Not needed anymore, goodbye, clean out your desk by Friday. Words broke through his fog of depression. They seemed to be coming from below, from the street.

"Jump! Jump! . . . Jump! Jump! . . . Jump! Jump!"

Professor Leon Mann in South Australia has studied this strange and repugnant expression of aggression, the suicide-baiting crowd. His analysis of twenty-one cases in which crowds were present when a person threatened to jump off a building, bridge, or tower is quite interesting. Crowd reaction, he suggests, may be primarily concern, or curiosity, or callousness. This last description is what characterizes the suicide-baiting crowd, in which its members jeer, taunt, and urge the victim to jump.

What are the conditions that give rise to such behavior? Professor Mann hypothesized that such a crowd would be characterized by what psychologists call *deindividuation*. This is a condition of diminished self-awareness, a condition in which, in a sense, one's identity is lost in and merges with the crowd. Deindividuation is more likely to occur under some circumstances than others, and the research sought to find out if these circumstances were present when there was baiting and absent when there was not.

■ **Crowd size.** People in large crowds should feel more anonymous than in smaller groupings. In fact, there was significantly more baiting of the victim in crowds of more than three hundred persons than in smaller ones.

■ **Cover of darkness.** Dim lighting should also contribute to deindividuation for the same reason as crowd size: it increases anonymity. Again, analyses showed more taunting, jeering, and encouragement to jump in incidents occurring after 6 P.M. than before.

■ **Physical distance between crowd and victim.** Where the potential suicide person is close to the crowd, making it difficult for crowd members to remain anonymous, little baiting should occur. Further, when the two are separated by so much distance that the victim would be unable to hear the taunts and jeers, it is also true that little baiting should occur. Most baiting should take place at an intermediate distance, when victim and crowd are far enough apart for crowd members to lose their identity, yet close enough for shouted communications to be heard. This is just what the research found: Baiting occurred only when the person threatening to jump was on the sixth to twelfth floors of the building involved, not at lower or higher levels.

■ **Duration of the incident.** It has been proposed that deindividuation is more likely when crowd members are tired and perhaps irritable. Consistent with this idea, baiting was substantially more frequent in those incidents lasting more than two hours as compared to briefer ones.

Like many other forms of aggression, suicide-baiting is hurtful and even cruel. The more such behavior can be understood, perhaps the better able we will become at preventing its occurrence—or at least minimizing its negative effects when it does take place.

3.

expressions
of aggression,
american style

Criminal Violence

Its Many Forms, Its Heavy Costs

The Journey to Crime

In trying to predict and control criminal behavior, it is valuable to understand the types of paths perpetrators follow in order to reach their victims. What is known about the actual journey to the crime site?

For most activities, people follow the "path of least resistance," the easiest route. Because knowledge about opportunities for a successful criminal act is usually greater the more familiar the criminal is with the location, one would expect the journey to be a short one, passing through streets the perpetrator knows well. This, in fact, is just what research has shown.

There is what criminologists call a distance-decay function, in which the number of crimes decrease the greater the distance from the criminal's residence. Although this ratio is generally true, it varies somewhat depending on the type of crime and the type of criminal.

The journey to crime for violent offenses is usually shorter than for property crimes. Perhaps because they typically are spontaneous crimes of passion, homicide and rape are the most localized crimes, often involving perpetrators and victims who live on the same block or even in the same building. In one study, victim and offender lived at the same location in 28 percent of rapes and 18 percent of homicides but in only 4 percent of robberies and 3 percent of vehicle thefts.

For another violent crime, aggravated assault, armed offenders traveled on average almost twice as far as those without weapons. The study also showed that for all the assaults combined, 47 percent took place within one-half mile of the offender's residence and 70 percent occurred within one mile.

Other researchers report a strong association between the distance traveled and the value of the property stolen in burglaries: The greater the value, the greater the distance.

In general, as far as the length of the journey is concerned, it is fair to say that there is a progression, with increasingly lengthy travel as one moves from violent crimes to vandalism to petty larceny to such long-distance offenses as drug crimes, fraud, and auto theft.

Who the criminal is also influences the journey to crime. Younger offenders are more likely to commit their crimes in their own neighborhoods than are older offenders. In fact, older offenders in one study traveled twice as far as younger ones, perhaps due to the differing nature of their respective crimes as well as to automobile availability. Male criminals travel farther than females; White criminals make longer journeys than do African Americans.

Finally, it is interesting to note that one researcher studying crime location found offense rates to be higher at the peripheries of the neighborhoods studied than at their centers. Perhaps criminals are prone to travel just far enough so that, on the one hand, they can minimize the risk of being identified and, at the same time, be able because of familiarity with the neighborhood to size up what is and is not a good opportunity for carrying out a successful crime.

Arson: Who Does It and Why

1827, an English chemist named John Walker invented the first friction match, and for the first time in humankind's centuries old use of fire there existed a widely available, easily used means for starting fires. Such use has typically been for better but not infrequently for worse. Fire warms us, cooks our food, and still drives much of our daily transportation as well as a good deal of our industry. Fire also destroys, and not a little of that destruction is intentional.

One recent estimate is that 25 to 50 percent of all fires begin by arson. It is a particularly costly form of criminal behavior, destroying billions of dollars in property and causing great damage in human death and injury. As with other forms of vandalism, perpetrators tend to be young—66 percent of all arsonists are under twenty—Caucasian, and male. As also seems to be happening for other crimes, females are becoming more active as perpetrators of arson. In 1965, there were twelve male arsonists for every female, the ratio was eight to one in 1983, and by 1993 it had dropped to six males for each female.

One expert has offered a psychological profile of the typical adult fire setter as a person of below average intelligence, with a history of poor performance in school. He comes from a large family, a harsh and unstable home environment, and has a troubled and inadequate social, marital, and employment history, often including drinking problems and prior difficulty with the criminal justice system.

Profiles of "typical" criminals for any crime are, of course, abstractions and not exact descriptions. In the case of arson, in fact, exact descriptions of typical perpetrators would be hard to come by because so many different types of arsonists have been mentioned by those who study it and try to prevent it. Thus, there are arson-for-profit setters, solitary fire setters, group fire setters, curious fire setters, revenge fire setters, the would-be-hero fire setters, the fire "buff" fire setters, the pyromaniacs, the excitement fire setters, the schizophrenic fire setters, child and adolescent fire setters, and the general arsonists.

Some of the types just listed are more common than others. In one study of arsonists in New York and California, for example, 52 percent report setting their fire(s) for revenge, 12 percent for excitement, others to cover up a crime, still others for no apparent reason.

As we noted above, a great deal of fire setting is done by young persons, especially young boys. One study showed that 45 percent of the boys studied had at some time engaged in fire play and that a third of these play experiences had resulted in a fire! At some level, interest in fire is almost universal among children, but healthy interest and damage-causing play are far from the same thing. Clearly, parents have a serious educational responsibility here. People who play with matches can indeed get burned.

I See It, I Want It,
I Take It

if aggression is properly defined as intentional physical or psychological injury to persons or property, perhaps it is not stretching things too far to view shoplifting as an aggressive act. Clearly, there is damage as a consequence of such theft behavior—to the business in which it occurs, to the other customers of that business, and often to the perpetrator himself or herself.

Persons committing this crime have been called, by one researcher, either *out of necessity* or *non-sensical* shoplifters. The first, for example, may be a poor, out-of-work parent stealing needed clothing or food. The second may be a middle- or upper-class individual, with ample funds in his or her pocket, stealing for perhaps more complicated reasons.

Non-sensical or not-out-of-necessity shoplifting may occur, one criminologist suggests, out of revenge against the store for real or imagined complaints, because of poor control of impulses, to help finance a drug or alcohol addiction, to somehow moderate difficult life stresses, or, in the case of adolescents and younger children, as a result of peer pressure and desire to win group acceptance. It has been estimated that about 90 percent of shoplifting is done by amateurs (known as *snitches*), and 10 percent by professionals (*boosters*).

Thus, as can be seen, all shoplifters are certainly not alike. Their motivations may indeed differ widely. Accompanying these motivations are a set of beliefs, heavily subscribed to by shoplifters in one study, that seem to "free up" or make easier the carrying out of the shoplifting:

- If I am careful and smart, I will not get caught.

- Even if I do get caught, I will not be turned in and prosecuted.

- Even if I am prosecuted, the punishment will not be severe.

- The merchants deserve what they get.

- Everybody at some time has shoplifted.

- Shoplifting is not a major crime.

- I must have the item I want to shoplift.

- It's OK to shoplift because the merchants expect it.

As the work of Charles Dickens and others portrays, shoplifting no doubt goes back as far as the initial shops and stalls that brought goods of different types together for purchase. Its seriousness as a costly and widespread crime, however, began with the opening of the first five and ten cent store by F. W. Woolworth in 1879 and reached full bloom as a 30-billion-dollar-a-year offense in America as, in recent years, the neighborhood mall became the community mall, then the regional mall, and now the megamall. Items stolen may be as inexpensive as food or drink consumed but not paid for while shopping (known as *grocery grazing*), to very expensive clothing, electronic equipment, or other costly goods. Perpetrators may wear the stolen item out of the store, conceal it under their clothing, or hide it in various props brought into the store (a booster box, a bad bag, a klepto bag).

Bring more and more people together, add movies (attracting teenagers), bars (attracting drinkers), and public transit stops (attracting nondrinking, low-income populations), and both motivation and opportunity have been brought together in a way that makes "I see it, I want it, I take it" more likely.

It has been estimated that only about one in thirty-five shoplifters are ever caught. That so many get away with it is rather surprising because businesses invest a great deal of energy, creativity, and money to combat shoplifting.

Some such efforts include physical changes in the way merchandise is packaged (large and unwieldy wrapping and boxing) or displayed (locked cabinets, inaccessible counters). Other efforts have focussed on various ways to increase the chances that perpetrators will be seen or caught in the act—or at least make them think that they will be seen or caught. These efforts include hiring more security and sales staff and training them in surveillance techniques; using in-store video cameras and aisle mirrors;

widening between-counter aisles to improve viewing of store customers; and regulating the number of customers occupying the store at any given time.

In addition to prevention and witnessing shoplifting as it occurs, a third approach is after-the-fact attempts to catch perpetrators with the stolen goods before they leave the store premises. Electronic price tags and various types of exit alarms are examples.

With all these varied human surveillance and high-tech approaches, why are so few shoplifters caught? There likely are many answers that involve customer traffic volume, store and merchandise layout, public relations, and more. But one answer concerns the high skill level plus low guilt level of many shoplifters. Two criminologists conducted a fascinating study that made this point very well.

Through various means, they hired two groups of persons for their experiment. One was a group of "novices," who reported that they had never committed an act of shoplifting. The other was a group of "experts," each of whom had done so at least one-hundred times, including at least ten times in the past year.

Each expert or novice was wired with a tape recorder and lapel microphone and was walked individually through a series of stores by the researchers. As they walked, they were asked to imagine that they were contemplating a shoplifting incident and describe all thoughts about it in their microphone.

An extensive analysis of these many comments about perceptions, feelings, strategies, tactics, and the like revealed that far more than the novices, the experts were highly focussed on the security and sales personnel and customers present, store layout, security devices, item size, and other aspects of "stealability." Novices, in sharp contrast, zeroed in not on the act but on the possible consequences of such behavior: arrest, trial, fines, jail.

So far, it looks like with this crime at least, the bad guys are winning.

Broken Windows,
Broken Dreams

In our great and growing concern in America today with aggression toward people, are we paying sufficient attention to aggression toward property? The two are, after all, close cousins. Aggression toward property takes many forms: the graffitied walls that increasingly comprise the corridors for America's streets; the abandoned and stripped cars parked thereon. It has been estimated that vandalism costs our 84,000 public schools more than 600 million dollars per year, broken windows being its most common expression, arson its most costly. For American business, the estimated annual cost of such intentional property damage is 1 billion dollars. In our forests and national parks, there are growing levels of damage and destruction of both the natural environment and campground facilities—cutting trees for firewood, garbage dumping, littering, cultural artifacts theft ("pot hunting"), soil erosion from all-terrain vehicles, cut fencing, grazing violations, graffiti, fires, and gunshot or other destruction of signs. This last vandalistic act, sign destruction, is also a major vandalistic cost on America's roads. About two million signs are replaced each year in the United States, 30 percent of them because of vandalism. One expert's estimate of the average life of a typical rural road sign: two years! Mass transit systems (cut seating, graffiti), libraries (book mutilation, arson), and museums (scratchings, breakage) are particularly common public targets of such illegal and often costly behavior.

Beyond substantial financial loss, aggression toward property may have an enormous human cost. The spray-painted initials, gang symbol, or hate message; the litter or trash blowing in the wind or collecting in a corner; the broken door; the knocked-over sign; the intentionally clogged and overflowing plumbing; and other damage, defacement, and destruction—each exact their price, in anger, in a sense of vulnerability, in fear of more of the same or worse to come.

What motivates aggression toward property? Psychologists have suggested three interesting theories to try to explain just why people vandalize. One theory stresses the seeking of excitement and challenge, mostly to overcome boredom. A second emphasizes the warped aesthetic enjoyment of destructive activity and its products. The third explains vandalism as a response to perceived unfairness, as an effort to regain control and, in a sense, square the account. From these and other speculations about why vandalism happens, many approaches to stopping or reducing it have been suggested and tried. Some target actual or potential vandals and by use of various combinations of education, publicity, punishment, and counseling try to change the vandal's desire to be destructive. Most approaches in use, however, aim not at such change in vandal *motivation* but instead at reducing or removing the *opportunity* to engage in vandalism by changing the physical environment in one or more significant ways. The main examples of this opportunity-reducing strategy are target hardening (toughened glass, slash-proof transit seats, concrete picnic tables), access control (locked gates, guard dogs, photo ID), deflecting offenders (graffiti boards, street detours), controlling facilitators (spray-paint sales control, removing construction site debris), exit-entry screening (metal detectors, closed-circuit TV), increasing surveillance (police and citizen patrols, informant hotlines, live-in custodial staff), target removal (use of graffiti-resistant surfaces, removal of pay phones and other targets), and removing inducements (rapid repair of vandalized property, use of small window panes).

The defacing of America continues. Vandalism is a blight on the landscape and on the cityscape. Many methods exist for changing both the vandal and his or her opportunity to deface and destruct. The more we use these methods, the better the environment in which we all live.

Vigilante Injustice

WE are all sick of graffiti; it insults us, it offends us, it frightens us. No matter that murder, assault, and other crime levels are mostly down a little; they *seem* to be going up—if not in actual amount then in plain awfulness, in randomness of victim, in vulnerability of locations. Many of us feel less safe, under siege, less able to control our own streets, homes, and communities. We avoid a favorite path in a nearby park, stay home some nights we'd prefer to be out, look uncomfortably over our shoulders as we pass through a run-down neighborhood, and fume at a world that feels so unsafe.

The police do the best they can, often at growing personal risk to themselves, yet to many they no longer seem to be the protective blue wall between "us" and "them" that we once felt them to be. So we arm ourselves to the teeth, pushing for more weapons, more lethal weapons, more concealed weapons, more killing bullets, and more freedom to employ our private armory where, when, and how we wish. The yesteryear myths of America's Wild West become more and more the realities of today.

In Los Angeles late one night, a citizen came upon two young men spray-painting graffiti on an overpass wall. What followed is in dispute, but in the end both men or *taggers*, were shot in the back, one fatally. The perpetrator, instantly labeled the "graffiti vigilante," quickly became a national folk hero, basking in prosecutorial forgiveness and community applause. Is this where we wish to head: the vigilante as hero? Is more, perhaps much more, vigilantism to come?

It certainly would not be the first time. Although citizens taking the law into their own hands has not been common in America in the last fifty years, during most of America's history vigilantism by individuals or groups was quite common. Whether one examines South Carolina's Back Country Regulators of 1767 (America's first vigilante group); the six thousand-member San Francisco Vigilance Committee of 1856; the eastern Montana group of 1884, considered the most violent American vigilante group; the 52 Texas vigilante groups of the nineteenth century, giving that state the distinction of having the greatest number of such groups; or most of the other 325 organized vigilante groups that have come and (mostly) gone since America began, it seems that certain common conditions cause them to appear and grow.

Vigilantism is more frequent in periods of economic uncertainty and social instability, when financial security seems threatened and preferred values are seriously challenged. In such times, many seek a "them" to blame it on, and convenient scapegoats are always near at hand: the Catholic, the Black, the Jew, the Latino, the immigrant.

Crime also figures heavily in the rise of vigilantism: its amount, its violence level, and how well or poorly authorities appear to have it under control. When crime rates seem to be rising, and police as well as other agents of the community's formal legal system are seen as ineffective, the need for self-protection, self-defense, and thus vigilantism finds fertile soil. Such economic and crime-control conditions have long been considered the common source of vigilantism.

What has changed, however, is just how vigilante behavior is carried out. The horse thief, counterfeiter, or land pirate targeted for vigilante aggression prior to the mid-nineteenth century would likely be given at least a half-serious trial, convicted, and then flogged and expelled from the community. After the 1850s, vigilante (in)justice turned both instant and lethal, and lynching became its frequent sentence.

America today is armed to the proverbial teeth. In the eyes of many, the social and community conditions that promoted vigilantism in the past are more and more with us today. The spirit of vigilantism is in the air. Will that dark period in American history, visited so often in the past, be revisited by us once again?

Fear of Crime

although about one in every 10,000 Americans will be murdered in any given year, approximately 2,200 of these 10,000 citizens worry about being murdered. When asked, "Is there any area around here—that is, within a mile—where you would be afraid to walk at night?" as part of annual national crime surveys over the past thirty years, between a third and a half of Americans express fear of their local community.

Whether measured by how many Americans are fearful at any given time, or how intense their fear is, or for how long they are afraid, fear of crime in the United States is quite substantial and quite a bit greater than the actual chances of becoming a crime victim.

For the majority of persons, how much they fear any particular crime is a combined result of how serious the crime is and how likely it is. Murder is very serious, but statistically quite unlikely. Receiving an obscene phone call is rather likely but is ranked as the least serious of sixteen crimes listed in a national survey.

Combining its seriousness and its likelihood, which crime is feared most? Having someone break into your home while you are away. Ranked second: being raped. Ranked third: being hit by a drunk driver while driving your car.

Females and older persons experience the most fear of crime. Only 7 percent of eighteen-to-twenty-year-olds but 41 percent of those over sixty report feeling very unsafe walking alone in their own neighborhoods at night. Six percent of the males reported such fear, but 23 percent of the females.

Although these differences in fear of crime seem to make sense—that is, aren't females and the elderly actually more vulnerable and therefore more likely to become actual victims?—the facts are otherwise. In what some criminologists call the *paradox of fear*, it has been shown that males and younger people are actually considerably more likely to become crime victims than are females and older persons.

Fear of crime is also greater among African-American citizens than Whites, persons living in urban areas than those in suburban or rural locations, and low-income families in contrast to middle- or upper-income.

Not all locations are equally feared as possible crime sites. In schools, youngsters are most fearful about restrooms, the schoolyard, and the hallways and feel safest in the classroom. City dwellers fear most their city's downtown, especially if it is peppered with graffiti, abandoned buildings, and drug trafficking.

Not only are some places feared more than others, some people are too. Young males are the most frightening when it comes to fear of crime, especially when they are in groups, and especially to females. Unfortunately, with regard to efforts to diminish racial stereotyping in America, some surveys show the fear of crime perpetration by young males is even greater if the males are African American.

What is a citizen to do? Some deal with their fear of crime by avoiding certain places, people, or activities. Some take precautions or protective steps: They travel by car, not on foot. Or they travel with others, not alone. Or they purchase and install locks, lights, alarms, or other devices. Or they follow what some have called insurance strategies: They carry little or no money and they insure or engrave property at home.

While avoidance, protection, or insurance may each in their own way help reduce fear of crime, use of each strategy changes who we are to some extent and, in a sense, makes us victims of the fear itself.

No one would argue against the wisdom of being prudent and aware as one goes about one's daily life. It will, however, make such daily living a lot more comfortable and less fearful if we all remember that the actual likelihood of becoming a victim of a serious crime is quite small indeed.

Domestic Violence

*Husbands, Wives, and Children:
Perpetrators in the Home*

The Home as a
Hitting Place

recent years, research aimed at trying to better understand and control aggression has gone beyond the study of perpetrators and victims to examine the locations in which aggression occurs. Where are crimes committed? Do different locations present different opportunities for aggression and even different outcomes?

Home is one of America's favorite hitting places. It is an opportune ground for small slights and major insults, where grudges can quietly smolder and violently flare, a private arena in which a self-appointed family dictator may take command, a tavern of sorts in which excessive drinking and lowered restraint can set a stage for violence, and a sheltered island in which aggression can let loose with little fear of punishment. It is also a physical structure and space often jointly occupied by potential aggressors and (literally) near-at-hand targets. Given all these aggression-promoting qualities, it is no wonder that more than 80 percent of the homicides in which offender and victim were from the same family take place at home.

The bedroom is the deadliest room in the house. Most acts of aggression occur when the perpetrator is very emotional, his or her anger level heightened. Bedroom-based arguments about sex, intimacy, and other volatile topics fit this picture exactly. In the bedroom, studies reveal, the perpetrator is most likely to be male, the victim female. The opposite is true in the kitchen, which is the second most frequent in-house location for both homicide and assault. Women are the usual offenders, males the victims. The living room is the next most likely location for aggressive behavior. Much of this site's violence appears to occur in front of, and to some extent in response to, television viewing. Conflicts over which channel to watch, or over differing reactions to program content, especially when the viewers have been watching shows depicting heavy doses of aggression, can readily light the fuse of domestic violence.

Interestingly, in one major study of the home as a hitting place, the only room in the house where there was no violence was the bathroom. The researchers described this room, which it should be noted usually has the only lockable inside door in the house, as often being declared a family refuge or a demilitarized zone!

What about burglary? Home is the place not only for aggression against persons but against property also. Research by criminologists has clearly shown that the homes within any given neighborhood do not have equal likelihood of becoming the target of a burglary.

In one fascinating study, the researchers were able to recruit thirty active burglars who individually rode along with the researchers to drive past and describe homes they had burglarized and those they had rejected as too high risk. Basically, the burglars made their decisions based on evidence of occupant (or neighbor) presence and potential gain. An expensive car in the driveway, a satellite TV dish in the yard, or other signs of good stuff inside, plus low likelihood of being seen—lights off all evening, newspapers and mail collecting, blinds drawn all the time, heavy shrubbery or fences between homes, few or no facing windows from other homes, little car or pedestrian traffic—these were the usual conditions for a "go" decision.

The burglars employed considerable creativity in these efforts to gauge possible gain and absence of occupants and neighbors. Their most common opportunity-estimating probe was simply to knock on the door or ring the doorbell. If anyone answered, the burglar simply asked for a nonexistent person or for directions. If no one answered, the burglary took place. Some noted the resident's name from the mailbox, left, looked up and called the resident's phone number, and left the phone ringing to return to the potential site. If the burglar could hear the phone still ringing, the house was judged unoccupied and safe to break into.

Another burglar put on jogging clothes, removed a piece of mail from the target's mailbox, and knocked on the door. If no one answered, the burglary took place. If someone did answer, the burgular said the mail had been found on the street and was being returned. One burglar, dressed conservatively, sought out homes next to those with a "For Sale" sign. Pretending to be a possible buyer, he walked around the yard of the for-sale house while estimating the likely success of burglarizing the house next to it.

Home may be a sanctuary, a respite, a nonviolent place to live, relax, relate, and more. But home may also be a hitting place, an often-unobserved location for assault or murder by those within, or a target location for the outsider seeking opportunities to intrude.

The Hitting Habit

america has the hitting habit. A few facts first: Between 4 and 14 percent of our children are physically abused (burned, bones broken, shaken severely, etc.). About one-third of these victims go on to become abusing parents themselves. Ninety percent of American youngsters are hit at least occasionally and often many times by their parents during their growing-up years. Three- and four-year-olds are hit the most, but one quarter of our children continue to be targets into their adolescence. Sons are hit more than daughters. Younger parents hit more than older parents.

Much is known about hitting in the American home, including its consequences. Any actions that appear to succeed are more likely to be repeated. Because the child being hit stops doing whatever he or she was hit for, at least temporarily, the person doing the hitting concludes that hitting works and is therefore likely to hit again. Furthermore, that person is not only more likely to hit the child but also to hit others. But what does the child learn? The data on pass-it-on hitting tell us that one important lesson to be learned from being hit is that "might makes right." Junior becomes that much more likely to be a hitter—an abuser, a bully, a fighter—himself.

In our own research on juvenile delinquency, we interviewed 250 incarcerated youths to learn what they thought caused so much aggression in America and what they believed could be done about it. Their theories of cause were similar to what criminologists believe: peer pressure, drug involvement, dysfunctional families. But when asked for solutions, almost to a person they gave very harsh answers, reflecting the way they themselves were consistently treated. Their suggestions for chronic aggression and delinquency: longer sentences, mandatory sentences, lock up the parents, life sentences, and the two champions for harshness, life sentence without food and lock up with an attack dog; if he moves, the dog goes for him!

A third problem with our heavy reliance on corporal punishment is that it fails to teach the target child a better way of responding when he or she feels frustrated or provoked. If being hit has any informational message in addition to "might makes right," it is to let the youth know what the hitter believes the youth did wrong. But it fails to instruct the youth how to do it right the next time.

We are not only proposing that hitting teaches the wrong lessons. We are also saying that if changing someone's behavior is its goal, it actually is inefficient. Research on the effectiveness of punishment shows it usually has only a temporary impact on changing behavior. Such research, in fact, demonstrates that whether or not such punishment works at all depends on many factors: who the punisher is, its consistency, its certainty, how quickly it follows the transgression, and more.

Hitting a child is a bad idea—as a corrective, as a lesson that only encourages the child's own future hitting, and on moral-ethical grounds also. Perhaps at some level many adults know this. Why else would they need to describe hitting by using such minimizing, palliative terms as *swatting, spanking* and *smacking* rather than the hitting, beating, and punching that corporal punishment of our children so often is.

There are several better ways to change children's behavior, ways that are both effective and humane. Time out in a quiet place for a few minutes to calm down an angry youngster is often a successful start. Losing a desired privilege or opportunity (such as in grounding) can serve as an effective corrective, as can insistence on restitution. Telling and showing a child the correct, proper, and desirable way to handle a situation provides the positive information that corporal punishment lacks.

In the last analysis, the best way to change children's behavior is to catch them being good. When a child is handling a difficult situation well, is behaving in a desirable and positive manner, we too often say and do nothing. After all, these are the ways he or she is supposed to behave. Such failure to reward positive behavior is a major parenting mistake. Behaviors rewarded are behaviors that continue. Praising desired behaviors is the very best way to have those behaviors become a regular part of a child's actions. Catch your children being good, and let them know it!

Parents Fight, Children Suffer

true, conflict is part of every marriage, good or bad. In some marriages, husband-wife differences are not major, or frequent, or the source of volatile anger. Some couples even use conflict constructively, to solve problems, grow closer, build their relationship.

Too often, however, conflict leads us down a destructive path, to anger, to bitterness, or to actual physical violence. When this happens, the price is often high not only for the husband and wife but for their children also. A great deal of research clearly shows that when parents fight, children suffer. In fact, if the aggression that flies between the couple is severe, half of the children will later show serious behavior problems. Witnessing parental violence can lead to consequences for the child that are as serious as if the violence were directed toward the child!

The effects may show up in behaviors that you can see, such as noncompliance, poor peer relations, vandalism, and increased aggression by the child toward peers, adults, and even toys. These consequences of parental violence are rather more common for boys than girls. Girls, in contrast to boys, frequently respond to marital fighting by anxiety, withdrawal, depression, and self-blame accompanied by shame and guilt. These unhappy reflections of parental violence on children's behavior can begin to show up as early as six months of age.

As these results of parents fighting suggest, the child can be hurt in two ways. Witnessing father and mother fight is a frightening experience. It makes the world seem dangerous, unpredictable, and out of control. Some children, in addition, feel responsible for the tumult. In addition to self-blame, shame, and guilt, they may try (even as toddlers!) to comfort and protect the parent, usually the mother. Older children may find themselves cast into the role of mediator, arbitrator, or even fight referee. There can indeed be serious long-term consequences for the child who, at an early age, is forced into the position of serving as parent to his or her parents.

Whether such behavioral, emotional, and long-term consequences for the child actually happen depends a lot on the nature of the parental fighting. Research has shown that the more frequent it is, the worse the impact on the child. Problems for the child, it has also been shown, are four times more likely when the marital fighting is physical rather than verbal. They are also considerably more likely when the content of what the parents are fighting about is the child himself or herself, as compared to any other topic.

But we need not be overly pessimistic here. As we noted earlier, couples can learn to deal with their differences in ways that are not harmful to themselves or their children, and may even be positive, constructive events. The good news is that, as parents learn to problem solve in positive ways, the earlier negative effects of their fighting on their childrens' behavior and emotional well-being have been shown to substantially decrease.

Murder as a Family Affair

 kill wives; wives murder husbands. Parents kill their children; children do in their parents. Murder is indeed often a family affair.

Almost 9 percent of all homicides are married-partner murders. When they happen, they often are no surprise to authorities. In one survey, in more than 80 percent of such homicides the police had been called to the home at least once during the two years preceding the incident and five or more times in half the cases!

Nine out of ten spouse murders occur in the home, usually as the culmination of a long and spiraling pattern of marital conflict. Men use a variety of weapons; 80 percent of the perpetrator wives use a gun. As is true for homicides in general, murder of a husband or wife is more likely on weekends than weekdays and in August and September as compared to all other months. Half of these crimes occur between 8 P.M. and 2 A.M. Many of the perpetrators, and almost as many of the victims, were drinking—often heavily—just prior to the killing. Murder in the family almost never happens without the prior warning of nonlethal violence between the spouses. Unfortunately, it is estimated that such violence is, in the case of later murdered wives, reported to the police in only a small minority of such instances.

Approximately one thousand children are murdered by their parents each year in the United States. When the murderer is the mother, it is more likely that she is single than married, younger than older. In fact, the younger the mother when she became pregnant, the more risk to the child. In turn, the child's greatest risk of being murdered by his or her mother is during his or her first year of life.

Fathers, in contrast, are more likely to kill older children, particularly their sons. Fathers are also much more likely than are mothers to murder all members of the family. Whereas most adult-to-adult killings are shootings or stabbings, murders of children involve a wider variety of methods, including beating with a blunt instrument, burning, smothering, drowning, and shaking to death.

When a child commits homicide, the victim is an acquaintance in half the instances, a stranger a third of the time, and, in 20 percent of the murders, a family member. The victims of girl murderers are twice as likely as those of boy perpetrators to be a family member.

More than 90 percent of the children who kill their parents have been abused by them, often severely. The killings, in a real sense, are often a desperate attempt at escape from an intolerable situation. In addition to such family violence, two particularly common characteristics of homes in which murder of a parent occurs are serious alcoholism or other substance abuse by one or more parents and the presence of firearms.

Husbands and wives may argue over sex, money, their relationship, childrearing, or what television show to watch. The argument may grow to a fight, the fight may lead to homicide. A parent may first scold a child, then hit, and later murder, for not listening, talking back, being sloppy, breaking promises, or, as in the case of one toddler homicide victim, not doing something (bowel control) that the child was in fact physically unable to do. A child may murder a parent for being denied certain opportunities (as in grounding), for being yelled at or hit by the parent, or in response to seeing the other parent being abused.

Family is or can be a place of warmth, security, intimacy, and love. It can also be a locus of conflict, sadness, hate, and homicide.

Sports Violence

*Violence and Nonviolence
on the Playing Field*

Sports Violence: Past, Present, and Future

Sports violence by both players and fans is as old as sport itself. Lethal combat between individual gladiators began at the first Roman Games in 264 B.C. and grew over the following decades to fights to the death among thousands of gladiators (and often spectators) at a time.

Boxing was first an event in the Olympic Games in 688 B.C. and, in its bare-knuckle form, continued as a popular spectator sport until 1860.

As the centuries unfolded, ever-new forms of sports violence emerged: wrestling, pankration (a boxing plus wrestling free-for-all), jousting (two knights riding at each other with iron-tipped lances), tournaments (groups of armored knights on horseback fighting with battle axes and massive swords), fencing (at first, with uncovered sword tips and no masks or vests), and bashing contests (known as cudgeling, back-swording, or quarter-staffing depending on the weapon).

Along with these several forms of violent sports over the ages involving human players, there has been centuries-long violent animal "entertainment." Cockfighting, perhaps the oldest violent animal sport, is still with us today in defiance of a 1976 federal ban against it. Dogfighting has also been popular for a long time, though its frequency has faded some in recent years. No longer much with us are baiting (fights between different animal species—dogs, bears, and bulls being the most popular), ratting, cat-in-a-barrel, pulling-the-goose, and similar vicious animal violence sports perhaps best not described in detail here. Currently, bullfighting and rodeo are two especially prominent forms of sports violence involving animals.

In case you doubt that rodeo fits in here, take the following, one-question test (pick one answer): The bull at the rodeo, with the rider on his back, jumps, twists, turns, bucks, and bellows because (1) he is so thrilled to be performing before an audience, (2) the two hundred–pound human on his back is a too-heavy burden he wishes to shuck off, or (3) the cattle prod used and bucking strap being yanked are exceedingly painful.

Sports violence is not some relic from a past age. It is still very much part of entertainment in America today, found in boxing, wrestling, football, soccer, hockey, not to mention basketball, baseball, and more. Football results in twenty-five to thirty deaths each year and many thousands of injuries. Hockey can sometimes look like boxing on skates. In these and other sports, many injuries, even deaths, occur at all age levels, peewee through high school, college as well as professional.

Such behavior expresses our obsession with winning, our machismo-driven fierceness especially when touched off by a controversial call by a referee, provocative mimed or verbal expressions of anger by a losing coach, or violence by other players on the field. Its frequent goals: intimidation, gaining respect, showmanship. Off the field and in the stands, spectator violence has also grown—directed at each other, at players, at those officiating the game. Such fan violence is especially likely when the stands are overcrowded, when there is physical access to the rival team's fans, when the alcohol has been flowing, and when the fans on each side have formed into singing, chanting, clapping, or cheering organized groups.

A lot more is known about sports violence. Members of home teams are more violent than those of visiting teams. There is more violence, regardless of which sport, when a team is in the middle of its league's standings rather than on the top or bottom. Teams wearing black uniforms are more aggressive.

As games progress and as seasons progress, sports violence increases; this fact is but one of dozens of research findings showing that behaving aggressively doesn't "get rid of it" (the catharsis idea). Instead, the opposite is true: Aggression, if it succeeds, causes more, not less, aggression.

Certain recommendations have been proposed. For players: Encourage positive interaction between opposing teams, such as end-of-game handshakes; praise and reward nonaggressive skilled performance; increase sanctions (fines, suspensions) for violent behavior; change equipment to increase player protection. For spectators: Play the national anthem after the game; have postgame concerts or a series of games or other events so that not all spectators leave at the same time; restrict the sale and use of alcoholic beverages; increase police presence. Less provocative coaching, more skilled officiating, and less sensationalizing media coverage will help too.

Put measures like these into play in America, and we will be able to avoid what has proven necessary in some European soccer stadiums—moats filled with water and steel fencing between rival groups of fans and between fans and the playing field—or games shown on television only, with no live audience at all at the stadium.

Play Fighting and Real Fighting: Is There a Connection?

Hank and Terry are two twelve-year-old classmates on a school trip to a local park. About 2 P.M., after a ballgame they both enjoyed, they are sitting next to each other on a park bench out of teacher view. Hank grabs Terry firmly but gently around the neck and, laughing, wrestles him off the bench as he verbally teases him for hitting into the game-ending double play. They roll on the grass, both now laughing. Terry winds up sitting on Hank as he tries to pin his arms to the ground. After five or so minutes of such horseplay, winded a bit and by mutual silent consent, they return to the bench, talking about the game, to sit and finish their drinks. Their play fighting has remained play fighting.

At more or less the same time, in the playground at the other end of the park, Sal and Benji, two nine-year-olds, have been taking turns along with changing groups of two or three other children in using the playground's slide. On this particular run, Sal goes first as Benji stands on the slide's top step waiting for Sal to clear the slide. Benji then sits at the top of the slide, ready to go. But Sal, rather than returning to the line, stands on the bottom of the slide and starts trying to run up it. Rising to the challenge, Benji shoves off, and the two meet in the middle of the slide. They continue down to the bottom, a laughing, shouting heap of arms and legs.

But they don't disengage at the bottom. At first, like Hank and Terry, they wrestle playfully. Shortly, their play hardens, becomes less playful. They become more intent on hurting each other. Kicks and punches are exchanged. Play fighting has become real fighting. A few minutes later a passing adult breaks up their fight. Sal walks away frowning, rubbing the bruise on his leg. Benji heads in the opposite direction, tissues pressed to his bloody nose. In the first scenario, what began as horseplay ended as horseplay. In the second, the play fighting became real, and the two youngsters were hurt. Which scenario, in reality, is more likely? Is there a connection between play fighting and the real thing?

Parents, teachers, and others concerned with children's behavior have asked the same question. When children in their charge wrestle, push, play kick, splash or dunk in the pool, or do other "rough and tumble" play, should they leave the kids alone? Is it part of normal, healthy development? Or is it a training ground for later aggression, to be stopped as soon as possible?

A few researchers have studied horseplay and its consequences. Boys do it more than girls, men more than women. Between men and women, there is more horseplay in close relationships than casual ones and more when one of the persons is a moderate or heavy drinker. No surprises here.

What of horseplay and aggression? Superficially, they look similar. But there are reliable differences. Play fighting or horseplay—in which the motivation is to have fun—involves smiling, often laughing, very few injuries, and the two persons remaining together afterward. It is game-like, often begins with an invitation, and participation in it may be declined by the child without losing face. Aggression—in which the goal is to hurt—involves a fixed gaze, frowns, injuries, and the parties going their separate ways after the fight. It often begins with an attack, consists of unrestrained blows, and, unlike play fighting, frequently draws an audience of other children. Compared to horseplay, real fighting involves more strength and, later, more regret. Children as young as four can tell which is which.

Does horseplay lead to aggression? Are those who play rough likely to be those who seek to hurt others? Research results are mixed. It seems quite probable that for children, the two are most often unrelated. Play is play; aggression is aggression. Two important exceptions have been identified, however: children who are frequently rejected by their peers; and chronically aggressive youngsters. These children are prone to errors when they try to read or decode the behavior of others, especially in falsely assuming hostile intentions by the other. Both of these types of children often find their rough play blending into serious aggression.

After puberty, the line between horseplay and hostility often gets fuzzier, at least for some adolescents and young adults. Two groups are especially prone to an increased blending of play fighting with real fighting: young males trying to build a macho reputation by displays of toughness; and young couples—especially those who have been dating a long time or are going steady—when one or both of them have consumed too much alcohol.

For the rest of us, horseplay may not only be transitory fun, there is some evidence that for most children it may even be valuable practice for the learning of a number of physical and social skills.

Nonviolent Games

starting in their earliest years, America's children grow up in a context of competition everywhere they turn. At home with siblings, at school with other students, at play in all kinds of games and sports, the mantra is compete, compete, compete. Theirs is a world that mimics, and many believe prepares them for, the adult world of business, dating, sports, and other forms of big-person competition.

Unfortunately, far too often the competitive activities of childhood and adulthood are transformed in actual practice to something meaner and more hurtful, namely aggression. Who has not seen or heard of, for example, a street game or an organized ball game or some other competitive play activity turning ugly and becoming an out-and-out fight?

There is an alternative—not widely known, or used, not very popular, yet a very good alternative. Nonviolent games, sometimes also known as cooperative games or noncompetitive games, exist in great numbers and apparently are great fun, say the relatively few children and adolescents who play them. These are games that also teach. They teach cooperation rather than competition, they teach playing to enjoy rather than playing to defeat, they teach that everybody can win and nobody loses.

How do these games work? As you read these rules, think about your own childhood and adolescent games and sports and you'll see just how different nonviolent, cooperative games are.

- Everyone who wishes to play can play. There are no tryouts to eliminate the less skilled.

- Everyone plays an equal amount of time, with equal opportunity to play each position via use of simultaneous games (multiball, multigoal) and frequent substitution when necessary.

- No goals are counted, no points awarded, no score kept.

- Players compete against their own past performance, not each other. Skill emphasis is on self-improvement.

- Extrinsic rewards (trophies, awards) are de-emphasized.

- There is active encouragement of cooperative skills; for example, all must touch the ball before a shot can be taken.

- There is expulsion from the game for intentional attempts to injure another player.

Some nonviolent games are cooperative versions of traditionally competitive ones; some are brand new games and sports. Hundreds of them exist. Here is a small sample.

For three-to-seven-years-olds:

- **Cooperative hide and seek.** Instead of having one player search for everyone else, everyone else seeks out one player. All players but one count to one hundred with their eyes closed, while the single player finds a hiding place big enough to hold everybody. Everyone then searches for the hider. Each one who finds the hider hides there too, until everyone is squashed into the hiding place.

- **Nonelimination Simon says.** Two games begin simultaneously, each with its own leader. If a player follows the leader after a "do this" with no "Simon says," that player transfers to the second game and joins in. There is no elimination from play, only movement between two parallel games.

For eight-to-twelve-year-olds:

- **Tug of peace.** People sit in a circle with a thick rope inside the circle at their feet. The ends of the rope are tied together. Everyone pulls at the same time so that the entire group can stand up together.

- **Long, long, long jump.** One child jumps, and a second child uses the place where the first landed as a jump-off place. Players, competing against themselves as they cooperate with each other, can attempt to better their total collective distance on successive tries.

For thirteen-to-seventeen-year-olds:

- **Blindfolded soccer.** Players on each team pair up. One of each pair is blindfolded and is the only one who can touch the ball. The other gives verbal instructions but cannot contact the ball. There are no goalies, and two balls are used. After a few goals, the members of each pair change roles.

■ **Boss, I can't come to work today.** This is a mutual storytelling activity in which players first pair up. Pair number one starts a sentence, such as "Boss, I can't come to work today" and then each player in turn expands the story by adding one or more words or phrases to the original sentence.

Our experience and that of others playing such games with children of all ages is that, first, they think the games (maybe we also) are quite strange. Their mind-set is to compete, not cooperate when playing. However, almost without exception, when you ease them into trying the game, they indeed enjoy it very much.

Competition often breeds aggression. Cooperation often breeds harmony. I strongly recommend nonviolent cooperative games.

School Violence

Aggression Comes to Class:
How to Keep It Away

The Ride to School:
Safe or Scary?

On a typical school day in America, 23,439,412 students climb onto 393,768 school buses for their ride to school. Together, the buses travel twenty-one million miles every day. For the vast majority of these children, the ride is a safe interlude of quiet time or of talking to a fellow student, joking, swapping stories, making plans. For a small but significant minority, it is a time for bullying, intimidation, vandalism, escalating horseplay, serious fights, or assaulting students or drivers. The school bus has become yet another location for aggression in America.

School districts are responding, often energetically and creatively. As parents and citizens, we all ought to know just what they are doing.

■ **Driver training.** Increasingly, the training of school bus drivers in the United States includes serious attention to managing the behavior of disruptive students. Psychological means for doing so, by skilled use of rewards and punishments, is appearing regularly in driver training courses, as is training in the physical skills necessary to intervene in a fight and restrain the combatants in a way that is safe for them, the driver, and the other students.

■ **Surveillance technology.** To aid in the apprehension (and conviction if necessary) of students causing trouble, and even more so as a device likely to discourage such trouble, school buses are with growing frequency installing surveillance video cameras set to scan and record student behavior. In part because such cameras are expensive devices, many districts have placed a camera box on every bus (each with a red light that is constantly on or flashing) but put an actual camera in only a portion of these boxes on a rotating basis. The commercial companies selling this equipment—Buscam, Silent Witness, Mobile Video, Eye Witness—each promote their wares as means to prevent aggressive behavior, catch the perpetrators, and prove to parents, school personnel, and legal authorities that such behavior took place.

■ **Ride alongs.** Just the driving part of driving a school bus can be a daunting and demanding task. To do so safely and responsibly requires of the driver both skill and full-time attention. To serve as behavior manager of dozens of students seated (or not seated!) behind the driver and out of his or her line of vision is often very difficult and not infrequently dangerous. In response, a number of school districts have added a second adult to the bus, a person responsible for such behavior management. This individual, working on a paid or volunteer basis, may be a guard, rider, monitor, parent, or aide. For many children, just the mere presence of such a person is enough to dampen likely aggressive behavior.

■ **Student sanctions.** When driver training, surveillance devices, and ride alongs are unavailable or insufficient, aggression-reduction sanctions may be directed toward students themselves. Students may be assigned seats so that when bus vandalism occurs, its perpetrator will more likely be identified. Apprehended school bus vandals may be required to provide restitution via money and/or bus-relevant (washing, cleaning) community service. In some states, if in the judgment of the bus driver the safety of riding students is being jeopardized, he or she is permitted to stop the bus, call for assistance, and have the offending youth or youths removed from the bus.

■ **School procedure.** In and around the school, and on the bus itself, added steps may be taken to deal effectively with student aggression. Bus behavior rules and consequences for misbehavior are being distributed to students and their parents each year and posted on all buses. School administrators and teachers may each do a ride along once or twice a year, both to help manage the students and to learn by experience about riding student behavior. An adequate number of teachers and staff may be deployed every day in the near-school area where and when buses arrive in the morning and leave at day's end. This milling around, waiting time can be an especially volatile and likely period for student aggression to erupt.

Working together, driver, rider, parent, teacher, and school administration can make the ride to school a safe and aggression-free trip.

Bullying: Schools' Not-So-Little Secret

Guns in school. Gangs in school. Drugs in school. Fights among students. We hear about these problems often. But what about the single most frequent expression of student aggression, bullying?

Bullying is the schools' secret, kept from others and even from themselves. Teachers and administrators often ignore it. After all, it doesn't usually disrupt the class, and besides, many adults mistakenly believe, it is a "natural" part of growing up. By enduring it, kids toughen up and are better prepared for life later on. Nothing could be further from the truth.

Bullies and their victims also keep it secret. The bully doesn't want to be punished; the victim fears reprisal. Victims also often feel pressure to deal with it on their own ("Be a big boy!") and believe no one will aid them if they do seek help.

More often than not, the victim's parents are unaware of the bullying. They may wonder why she comes home during the school day to use the bathroom, or how his clothing got torn, or why she seems so hungry at supper (her lunch money was extorted earlier).

Just what are the facts, and what can be done to make this frequent and nasty behavior more public and less damaging?

Several experts estimate that between 15 to 20 percent of all school-children are regularly bullied. The bullying may be verbal, such as threats, insults, teasing, starting rumors about the person, or trying to isolate or intimidate him or her. Often it is physical: pushing, tripping, kicking, hitting.

About two-thirds of the bullying is by boys and quite often is physical. Bullying by girls is usually more covert: such as gossiping, shunning, and the like.

Bullies tend to be hyperactive, domineering, impulsive, attention-seeking boys with little empathy for the feelings of others. Frequently, they bully not only fellow students but teachers, parents, and siblings also. They often come from homes in which the parents were (and frequently still are) bullies themselves. They commonly are parents who are strong believers, and users, of corporal punishment, yet are quite inconsistent in how they discipline, sometimes very strictly, sometimes very permissively.

Being a bully is bad for its victims but for the bully also. Research shows, for example, that elementary school bullies are very likely to grow into antisocial adults with few friends, poor marriages, and trouble with the law. One study, on this last point, revealed that 60 percent of the bullies in grades six through nine had at least one criminal conviction by age twenty-four!

The victims, sometimes known as whipping boys or hostility sponges, are typically physically weaker children, socially insecure, frequently anxious, often lonely and abandoned by other children. As one school expert put it, they sit small in their seats. To the bully, such behaviors and demeanor signal that the person is an easy mark, unlikely to retaliate.

Since it so often is a hidden event, happening most commonly on a playground, or in a school corridor or other site with low adult supervision, the bullying may continue for a long time, even years. Its consequences are several and often severe. Its chronic target will often suffer in academic performance and increasingly avoid people, places, and even school itself (truancy and dropout are not unusual). As it becomes more extreme, the victim may begin bringing a weapon to school or seek to join a gang for protection. At its most severe, suicide or homicide may occur.

A good start in dealing effectively with this widespread form of aggression is any and all steps to bring it into the open. We have to first seek it out in order to root it out.

School administrators and teachers should plan and carry out a zero-tolerance policy for bullying. Announce what it is, why it is wrong, why it won't be tolerated, and what (nonviolent) punishments will be used with all who bully. Just as with good parenting, schools need to set a climate of positive adult involvement and firm limits on unacceptable behavior.

A few weeks into any school term, and usually before the teacher knows it, most of the children in the class know who the class bullies and victims are. A bullying hot line, as used in Japan, or the creation of a "telling school" (where reporting serious aggression is urged as the school norm), as in England, both sound like workable ideas transportable to America.

Eighty-five percent of schoolchildren are neither bullies nor victims, but they can certainly help reduce it, not only by informing adults when they see it but also by being urged to welcome and include those students who are chronically left out of play and work activities.

Bullying is bad business: for the victim, for the bullies, for all of us. Let's get it out in the open, and start dealing with it. Every student has the right to learn in a safe environment.

Sexual Harassment
Comes to School

aggression is usually
defined by those who study it as intentional physical or psychological injury. By this definition, sexual harassment certainly qualifies as aggression. It is a form of aggression that is common in its occurrence and serious in its consequences, and it is taking place at younger and younger age levels.

In a recent large survey, about half the boys and as many as two-thirds of the girls ages eight to eleven reported being the target of sexual jokes; having sexual rumors spread about them; or actually being touched, pinched, or grabbed in a sexual way. These are youngsters just barely beginning to experience the hormonal changes usually associated with the start of interest in the opposite sex—a bad time indeed to begin learning that too often sex and aggression frequently go hand in hand.

The same survey made quite clear that the consequences of being a regular target of such sexual harassment are not minor. About a third of the girls and a sixth of the boys report difficulty in paying attention in class. They become less frequent contributors to class discussions and say they do not want to come to school altogether.

The effects of sexual harassment go beyond academic performance to seriously affect the emotional life of these children. About two-thirds of the targeted girls and a third of the boys say they are more self-conscious, less self-confident, often embarrassed, and frequently afraid in school.

We tend to think of sexual harassment as behavior perpetrated by adult males—employers, politicians, professors—toward adult females. Its range, however, is considerably broader and as we have seen often includes children harassing other children.

Unfortunately, sexual harassment is almost always a hidden act, one rarely seen by others and unlikely to be revealed by either perpetrator or victim. As parents, teachers, or other responsible adults, we have an obligation here not to shut our eyes. We have gotten used to thinking about sexual harassment as an inappropriate behavior by adults. We cannot afford to maintain the fiction that our children are not also its targets.

Guns Go to School

the cartoon made the point with a punch: Titled "Back to School Supplies," it shows a young adolescent on his way to school, knapsack slung over his shoulder, notebook and ruler sticking out of its top, pencil tucked behind his ear—and a .357 magnum revolver stuck in the waistband of his pants.

Is the situation really that bad, or are a small number of incidents causing far more concern than their numbers deserve? The facts, it seems, lie somewhere between.

More than 95 percent of our children go to school each day without a gun or any other sort of weapon, and most of them do so because their schools are safe, nonthreatening places.

Some children do bring weapons to school, mostly claiming they do so for protection. What weapons? Their variety is remarkable: weighted gloves, stun guns, steelies (in a bag), brass knuckles, auto batons, bayonets, bats, screwdrivers, box cutters (a metal detector-avoiding recent favorite), knives, and guns.

Guns have clearly caused the most concern, to the government, now seeking to declare legal gun-free zones around schools; to parents, fearing a goodbye on a school morning may be a goodbye forever; to school authorities, scrambling to find ever more effective ways to keep guns off the premises; and to students, the potential victims, fearful of attack in numbers well beyond actual frequency.

What are the facts surrounding gun use in school? About two-thirds of the youths bringing guns to school got their arms from a friend or family member. Though in general there is more school violence in junior rather than senior high school (seventh grade is the most aggressive grade), approximately two-thirds of the gun-use incidents in American schools take place in senior high schools.

Although some guns are fired by accident in schools (13 percent of all incidents), 65 percent are intentional shootings. Why does one student intentionally shoot another? Where and when these shootings occur provides ample clues to their motivation.

Although students spend at least 90 percent of each school day in classrooms, three-quarters of the shootings in recent years took place elsewhere: the school yard, the parking lot, the cafeteria, athletic facilities, and, by far the favorite shooting ground, the hallways. While 22 percent of the shootings took place during classes, 32 percent occurred in the four-minute transition periods between classes.

Most classes are times of attention to lessons, restricted movement, and high levels of teacher supervision. Between class transitions are, for too many students keenly oversensitive to imagined insults, times of attention to "bad looks," "stare-downs," or "intentional" bumps from students passing the other way. These incidents occur in a context of lowered teacher supervision, to youngsters set to respond not with counter-insults or even their fists but instead with the metal equalizer weapon in their pockets or book bags.

In addition to such real or imagined insults, students have shot other students in schools over rights to drug-selling turf or romantic disagreements, as a culmination of racial disputes, and in fights over material possessions—jewelry, coats, and Walkmans.

What are schools doing in response? Increasingly, expulsion is their answer, or at least suspension for long periods, perhaps with reassignment to special, alternative schools.

Many things are also being done to schools themselves in the effort to make them gun-free. Metal detectors are the most frequent change thus far. That they are of value is clear; that not a small number of weapons (including guns) still enter the building is also clear, as is the fact that such devices can indeed change the climate of a school, making it more prison-like.

Clear mesh book bags, locker searches and locker removal, weapons hot lines, and car searches are all also increasingly being used.

Our schools most definitely are not becoming armed camps. Yet the era of the school as neutral territory, a uniformly safe place for learning with no threat to its students beyond an occasional fistfight or wrestling match, is over. Bringing weapons to school, including guns, is still a rare event for the vast majority of students. Nonetheless, it does happen and is happening with increased frequency. Government, school authorities, parents, and students are wise to be concerned, and to continue their use of prudent responses.

School Dress Codes and Uniforms: What's a Student to Wear?

In recent years, two kinds of aggression relating to students' clothing have become more and more common in America's schools.

Physical aggression—punches, knifings, shootings—have been reported, especially in gang-infested secondary schools, when a student wearing the "wrong" color shows up at the wrong place at the wrong time. In some instances, the assaulted student has been a member of a rival gang wearing a bandanna, jacket, beads, or other item in his own gang's colors. In other cases, aggression over clothing may have nothing to do with a gang. One adolescent may be wearing an expensive jacket or a piece of jewelry that another student wants and be assaulted for it in what is best described as an in-school mugging.

Other times, the victim has also been a nongang member, ignorant of his school's unwritten clothing color codes, who simply wore the wrong thing to school that day.

Psychological aggression—teasing, harassing, belittling about clothing worn or not worn—is also more common, even at the elementary school level. Commercial advertising directed toward younger and younger children, as well as peer pressure to "dress right" ("Are you wearing Kmart clothing *again?*"), have made youngsters increasingly aware of the difference between whatever is the current "in" fashion and (often low-priced) out-of-step clothing.

The first type of aggression is usually easily spotted; the second type is typically well hidden. Both are hurting America's schoolchildren.

With a frequency that I believe will only continue to grow in spite of legal challenges in some communities, schools are responding in two ways. They are telling students, by means of dress codes, what they are not permitted to wear; and, sometimes in the very same schools, they are requiring that school uniforms be worn and denying admission to the school when they are not.

Items frequently prohibited by school dress codes today include

- Gold jewelry or dental caps

- Baggy pants

- Bandannas

- Pants with elastic ankle gathers (a great place to hide a weapon)

- Underwear worn as outerwear

- Doc Martens combat boots (common skinhead footwear)

- Selected team jackets and caps (sometimes of particular colors)

- Drug message or vulgar T-shirts

- Tanktops, halters, see-through blouses

School uniforms, the second solution, have long been common in many of the private and parochial schools in America, and now a growing number of public schools are trying them on as well.

It is common that when new programs of any type begin, the early reports of their effectiveness are positive. Such is the case for school uniform programs. They may or may not reduce aggression and have other benefits in the long run, but for now, both teachers and administrators speak glowingly of less jealousy, less competition, less bullying, more order, more identification with the school, and a greater sense of community.

Maybe the next step will be having teachers and school administrators wear the uniforms too!

The Low-Aggression
Classroom

We all know or can imagine what a classroom full of aggression looks like: Noise, movement, disruptiveness, horseplay, shoving, hitting, bullying, harassment, and, now and then, an out-and-out fight or an assault on the teacher.

What about the low-aggression classroom? What does that look like?

Physically, it has several features. Each child has his or her own desk or space. The aisles are wide enough to be "traffic friendly," making bumps and congestion less likely. The teacher's desk is well placed, so that the entire room can be seen. The room has personal touches here and there, to reflect a sense of "this is our room" to the students.

As we watch the teacher teach, we notice certain qualities. The material is presented in an interesting way and seems relevant to the needs and interests of the students. There is very little "down time" or empty time. Teaching moves along at a steady pace, and the shifting from one topic to another goes smoothly.

The teacher seems able to keep the entire class involved and paying attention. When there is a disruption, misbehavior, or aggression by one or more students, the teacher responds swiftly, fairly, and firmly. Punishment when given is not excessive but is strong enough that the student understands it is a punishment.

Classroom rules and procedures are made clear from the beginning. When work is well done, and rules are followed, they are frequently and generously praised by the teacher. Discipline and learning are promoted not just by "sticks" but by "carrots" also.

There are other noticeable qualities of the teacher, the teaching, and the climate in a low-aggression classroom. In numerous ways, the teacher gives the students a "can do" message, letting them know that success is both expected and possible. To promote such success, the teacher uses different teaching methods for different students, trying to match how lessons are delivered with each student's best learning style.

In our increasingly diverse society, students from several ethnic groups may make up the class. Rather than being ignored or perceived as an obstacle, this student diversity is emphasized by the teacher in the low-aggression classroom, enhanced, and transformed into something that enriches the class.

Parents are involved. In numerous small and not so small ways, a helpful level of collaboration between home and school is developed. To a meaningful degree, the school belongs to the community. It becomes a jointly owned place for learning and academic achievement, not fighting and academic failure.

We hear a great deal these days about school violence and conjure up images of a public education system near collapse. We need to remind ourselves that such a picture is more often the exception, not the rule. By far, American children in most American school systems go to school safely every day, learn their lessons reasonably well, and do so in low-aggression classrooms.

Teaching Prosocial Behavior to Antisocial Youth

I t may be wistful fantasies about bygone times, but a great many Americans believe that compared to the typical youngster of decades past, today's child and adolescent is ruder, more self-centered, less self-sufficient, less future-oriented, and, in a variety of ways, more aggressive.

Comparisons with the past may or may not be accurate. However, what clearly is accurate is that a very great many such socially unskilled young people do exist in the United States today. Perhaps home, church, and school did a better socializing job back then. Perhaps harried families, overburdened and underfunded schools, high levels of mass media violence, and a general "me first" orientation to America are among the shapers of today's socially skill-deficient youngsters.

Whatever the causes, many experts have noted that children and adolescents are often weak or lacking in such positive or prosocial skills as using self-control when needed; helping others; negotiating differences; expressing affection; or responding nonviolently and constructively to such challenges as teasing, accusations, failure at a task, embarrassment, or group pressure.

Somehow, it seems, many such getting-along skills were informally taught to many of us, perhaps by adult models competent in such abilities, as we grew up; no formal teaching of them was necessary. But now this need does exist, so there are a number of social skills training programs actively being used in schools, agencies, community centers, and other sites where young people gather.

Our own training and research group has developed one such approach, called Skillstreaming, now in use in hundreds of youth-oriented settings across America. It is being applied to many different types of youngsters but especially to those with aggression problems. Small groups of such children or adolescents are brought together and 1) shown several examples of expert use of the behaviors making up the skills in which they are weak or lacking (i.e., modeling); 2) given several guided opportunities to practice and rehearse these competent interpersonal behaviors (i.e., role playing); 3) provided with praise, reinstruction, and related feedback on how well their role playing of the skill matched the expert model's portrayal of it (i.e., performance feedback); and 4) encouraged to engage in a series of activities designed to increase the chances that skills learned in the training setting will endure and be available for use when needed in the school, home, community, institution, or other real-world setting (i.e., transfer training).

Using these four procedures, a curriculum of up to fifty skills are taught, most of which are prosocial, positive alternatives to using aggression. Two examples:

Skill 18: Dealing With Someone Else's Anger

Step 1. Listen to the person who is angry. Don't interrupt; stay calm.

Step 2. Try to understand what the angry person is saying and feeling. Ask questions, get explanations, restate them to yourself.

Step 3. Decide if you can say or do something positive to deal with the situation. Listen, be empathic, correct the problem, ignore it, or be assertive.

Step 4. If you can, choose one alternative and do it.

Skill 42: Dealing With Group Pressure

Step 1. Think about what the group wants you to do and why.

Step 2. Decide what you want to do. Yield, resist, delay, or negotiate.

Step 3. Decide how to tell the group what you want to do. You could give reasons, talk to one person only, delay, or assert yourself.

Step 4. Tell the group what you have decided.

By means of demonstration, rehearsal, feedback, and practice, people are successfully taught how to drive a car, sink a foul shot, speak a foreign language, and many other types of skills. Years of research have now shown that a wide variety of skill alternatives to aggression can effectively be taught the same way.

Gang Violence

Serious Violence From the Peer Group

A Short Course on Gangs

there are now approximately five thousand juvenile gangs in the United States, involving about 250,000 youths. Some 235,000 of these are males, 15,000 females. These last numbers have progressively changed in recent years so that although boys outnumber girls about fifteen to one, the number of girl gang members has steadily grown. While they still join later and leave earlier than the boys, they have become more independent of them, and, as are the boys, they are clearly becoming increasingly violent.

Up until the mid-1970s, almost all youth gangs were neighborhood-based, turf-defending youngsters, their ethnicity homogenous within each gang, whether White, African American, Latino, Asian, or otherwise. Now about a third of such gangs are "business" (drug) oriented, less concerned about neighborhood, and often of mixed ethnicity within the gang. Gangs have become, in a sense, equal opportunity employers!

Youths are recruited into gangs through friendship with members, because it may be a family or community tradition and expectation to belong, and sometimes coercively—as when the so-called neutron (a nonmember youth living in the neighborhood but uninterested in the gang) or a "peripheral" (a nonmember who occasionally interacts with gang members) is forced into membership under threat of reprisal for refusing.

What motivates youngsters to join a gang? They join for friendship, to have a source of pride and self-esteem, to feel part of a group, to help develop their own identities, for excitement, for access to resources. Note how all of these reasons for joining are normal, typical, and even healthy adolescent motives. They are the very same reasons that nongang adolescents join athletic teams, social clubs, or other youth groups. The motives of prospective gang members are fine. How they seek to satisfy these goals is another matter.

Most of the time, gang members just "hang out"and engage in those several types of activities considered typical for adolescence. Much of this behavior is devoted to enhancing the tightness and solidarity of their group and their difference from other gangs. "Us" versus "them" is a major theme of their daily lives, as reflected in their heavy use of hand signs, graffiti, clothing with gang logos, ways of wearing clothing, and other means for "representing" and "signifying." Unfortunately, for some, a good bit of time and energy is spent less benignly, in such illegal activities as drug selling, protection, arson, mugging, gambling, and violence.

Gang violence, in particular, has become a focus of serious concern. It may take several forms. Although the fair fight and the rumble of yesteryear seem to have faded, the armed foray (drive by, show by) into a rival gang's neighborhood has become more frequent.

Also increasingly with us are "turning" (a violent initiation of new members), "wilding" (an unorganized marauding along a street or elsewhere), and "swarming" (breaking into a home to steal, threaten, and assault). Younger gang members often are violent in order to build a reputation; older members seem more interested in aggression for purposes of material gain.

What happens to gang youth as they grow older? Some, but fewer than in the past, age out, marry out, or job out into the legitimate economy. Some remain in the gang well past their juvenile years, especially in drug-involved gangs. Others move on to careers in individual or organized crime. Many go to jail. A distressing number die.

America's future success in dealing with juvenile gangs, in minimizing their numbers and criminal activity, does not look bright. There are twenty-five million persons in the United States today aged thirteen to twenty-one. By the year 2010, thanks to the "echo boom" children of the baby boom, there will be more than thirty-one million such persons. Thus, a growing pool of individuals from which gangs may grow exists.

What other ingredients are necessary for our prediction of a growing gang problem to actually materialize? Many of this increasing number of potential members need to grow up in a society that constantly displays aggression (especially *successful* aggression) in its homes, streets, schools, and mass media. This most certainly is an accurate description of America today. Further, for such youngsters to actually behave violently once recruited to a gang, enough lethal weaponry must be available. The 220 million privately owned guns in the United States are a great start at solving that problem!

Finally, this large number of aggression-trained and adequately armed youths will join gangs and behave violently if there is a lack of adequate places and resources for them to meet the normal, legitimate, adolescent needs discussed earlier. For many gang-prone youngsters, such needs can be met by exactly the kinds of social, recreational, vocational, and educational programs mistakenly labeled as *pork* by recent crime bill opponents. For success in helping to minimize ganging in America, such programming is essential.

Gang Violence: Forms and Functions

many of the approximately five thousand juvenile gangs in the United States seem to be becoming more violent. What they do, and where and when they do it, depends on a number of factors.

Aggression within a gang, that is, toward members of one's own gang, in the vast majority of instances is verbal—criticism, cursing, ribbing, put-downs, insults in fun and insults for real.

Physical violence within a gang is much less common and usually happens as part of initiation into membership (turning in), for failure to follow important gang rules (such as regarding drug selling or use or having sex with a fellow member's relative), or for trying to resign from the gang at a time the gang deems premature.

Physical attack on a member of a rival gang, or upon strangers, is in contrast rather more frequent and can take several forms. When the fictional Jets and Sharks of *West Side Story* met in the school yard to fight it out primarily with fists, sticks, and similar nonlethal weapons, the gang rumble became a fixed piece of American mythology.

In reality, the rumble was quite far from a common event. Although such fights between rival gangs did happen, as often as not some last minute, face-saving event took place to prevent them—a flat tire, an anonymous call to police, a mix-up about the correct location for the fight.

Also largely gone from the current gang violence scene is the fair fight, in which a member representing each gang, usually the leader or his "war lord," fight it out with their fists until one gives up, surrenders, or signals "enough!"

Today, gang violence is both different in form and far more lethal. In its most publicized expression, a clique or subgroup of a gang conduct a foray. This is an automobile excursion into a rival gang's neighborhood either to flash weaponry in order to intimidate (the *show by*) or use weaponry in order to injure or kill (the *drive by*).

Most commonly, drive bys are directed toward whatever gang occupies the adjacent neighborhood. They may begin from a real or imagined insult, a bad look, a rumor, ethnic tensions, a dispute over turf rights, or, most commonly, a macho expression of "us" versus "them." Increasingly in recent years, such high-level violence has grown from conflict over drug-selling rights.

In a variety of forms, gang violence is also being directed toward innocent citizens going about their daily business and not only those caught by chance in the cross fire of a drive-by shooting. In what has been called *wilding*, a large number of gang members maraud down an avenue, breaking a window here, assaulting an elderly citizen, stealing a purse, creating mayhem. The infamous case of the Central Park jogger, the young woman attacked, raped, and beaten senseless by a marauding gang in the New York City park, is an example of wilding.

Swarming is another form of gang violence toward uninvolved citizens. Also called *home intrusion*, it began in Toronto among the Vietnamese population there, often believed to be persons who by custom were distrustful of banks and preferred to keep their savings in their home. A knock on the door at night, opened by the homeowner, and a dozen or more gang members swarm in to threaten, steal, intimidate, and injure.

On a recent trip to an Asian country in which motor scooters are quite popular, I came across yet another form of gang violence, *slashing*. A group of juveniles cruise on their scooters on a city street past pedestrians. With no provocation, one reaches out as he drives by and slashes at a pedestrian with a knife. A counterpart to such random violence has recently been reported in the United States. Labeled *bashing*, one of a group of gang members in a cruising automobile leans out its window, baseball bat in hand, and smashes the bat against the head of a passing citizen near the street.

Foray, show by, drive by, wilding, swarming, slashing, bashing: Gang violence in our country and beyond is growing. We should all indeed be concerned.

Gang Graffiti: What's the Message?

graffiti more and more frequently blemishes our urban neighborhoods. Although some of it is from the taggers seeking to flood their streets with their stylized initials or so-called street art, much comes from the hands of juvenile gang members. What is their message?

Just as "Posted, No Trespassing" signs are commonly used by rural property owners to mark the boundaries of their land and warn off outsiders, graffiti consisting of a gang's name (and perhaps logo) seeks the same purposes in city settings.

"This is our territory," it tries to proclaim, "we own it, we will defend it, so stay out!" While such graffiti is likely to appear all over the neighborhood claimed by the gang, it may be most frequent around the boundaries defining the neighborhood, just like the rural "Posted" signs.

Neighborhood-protecting gangs often paint not only the name of the gang in their graffiti but a list of all the members too. Sometimes this listing of member monikers or nicknames is in order of status within the gang.

In San Diego recently, a smart detective used this listing to catch a murderer. A gang had put up graffiti of its name and members. The police, following recommended practice ("the three R's"), read it, recorded it, and removed it. That night, a murder took place. The next day, the gang's graffiti reappeared, but a member listed eighth the first time was now listed second. The detective correctly guessed that the youth showing this rapid rise in status was their murderer!

Along with territorial marking, gang graffiti may be used for more openly hostile purposes, such as issuing a challenge or "giving notice" to a rival gang. One Crip gang in Los Angeles, for example, included B/K in its graffiti, for Blood killer.

Any Blood gang member who comes along is likely to respond to such hostility either with aggressive graffiti actions of his own (for example, cross out the original Crip graffiti or redraw it upside down as a message of disrespect) or with more direct aggressive actions, such as a drive-by shooting.

Graffiti may also be used to communicate more benign messages, such as with the "wall of heaven." This is a sometimes elaborate drawing of the names of all deceased gang members, usually with the initials R.I.P. (Rest in Peace) under each.

Or, again, to disrespect the deceased members of a rival gang, their names may be drawn upside down on what has been called a "wall of hell."

When you pause to think about it, a criminal or semicriminal organization publicly and widely advertising its presence and membership is strange behavior. It is "here we are, come and get us" help for the police. Clearly, this is why those gangs that have gone heavily into the drug business (perhaps a third of America's nearly five thousand juvenile gangs) are using graffiti less and less.

4.

who and where? perpetrators, victims, and places

Perpetrators

Who Commits Violence and Why

Multicide: Mass Murder, Serial Murder, Spree Murder

homicide involving a number of victims may take different forms. Let's get them straight. Mass murder is the killing of three or more victims at one time and in one place. Serial murder is the killing of three or more persons, almost always in different locations with more than thirty days passing between the first and last killings. Spree murder, also involving three or more victims, occurs within a thirty-day period, usually in combination with the commission of a felony, most often robbery.

Mass murderers often, but serial and spree killers seldom, die at the scenes of their crimes. Criminologists have identified five types of mass murderers:

- *The disciple* kills as directed by a charismatic leader, such as Charles Manson or Jim Jones at Jonestown in Guyana. The victims (usually strangers), the method, the time and place are chosen by the leader; the murders then are carried out by the disciples.

- *The family annihilator* is a mass murderer who kills an entire family. Quite typically this killer is the family's senior male figure, often a person with a serious drinking problem.

■ *The pseudocommando* is often preoccupied with weaponry, stockpiling various arms and using them in a mass murder event typically carried out to gain maximum attention for a cause, an issue, or a protest. Charles Whitman killed sixteen persons in this manner, shooting indiscriminately from a tower on the University of Texas campus.

■ *The disgruntled employee* retaliates for real or imagined wrongs at his or her place of current or past employment. Victims may be the employer or co-workers, seen by the perpetrators as the source of their troubles, or random employees or customers who chanced to be at the wrong place at the wrong time.

■ *The set and run killer* plants a bomb (set to explode after his or her departure) or poisons food or medicine on store shelves (to be sold later). The bombed federal building in Oklahoma City and the Tylenol poisoning attempt are respective examples. The intended victims may be innocent building occupants or store customers unknown to the killer, or the owner of the bombed building or store.

For many decades, serial killings were almost exclusively a crime perpetrated by males. In recent years, there has been a significant increase in serial killing by females, paralleling the general increase in women's participation in violent crime.

Women's serial murder crimes, however, tend to be less overtly violent than those perpetrated by males; women prefer to use poisons rather than (as with the males) firearms. Much more frequently than is true for males, they may know their victims and be killing for what criminologists call "comfort" reasons: money, insurance benefits, business gains. Most are White and tend to be in their early thirties when their serial killings begin.

Whereas in the typical homicide offender and victim know each other and often are close relatives, in male serial murders, the victim (like the mass murder victim) is usually a stranger victimized by chance. Jack the Ripper, David Berkowitz, Ted Bundy, and Jeffrey Dahmer are well-known perpetrators of this type of homicide. Criminologist Ronald Holmes at the University of Louisville, a renowned expert on this topic, estimates that at any one time there may be as many as two hundred serial killers on the loose in the United States.

Some male serial killers are widely nomadic, perhaps in an effort to avoid arrest. Others, often more likely to be apprehended, are geographically stable. Regardless of their mobility pattern, Professor Holmes suggests four types of such individuals:

■ The *visionary* kills in response to hearing voices or seeing visions insisting that he or she kill certain people or types of people. Such auditory hallucinations and visual delusions, for these individuals, are powerful directives they are unable to resist.

- The *mission* serial killer acts not from voices or visions but instead from a self-imposed duty to eliminate persons or categories of persons he or she deems to be undesirable.

- The *hedonistic* serial killer is described as a thrill seeker, killing for sexual excitement. Not uncommonly, after the murder, this type of perpetrator commits further aberrant acts upon the corpse, such as sexual behaviors or dismemberment.

- The *power/control* serial killer is motivated by an overwhelming need to dominate. Having complete control of the victim, culminating in the homicide, excites and gratifies him or her.

Multiple murders, mass, serial, or spree, are statistically rare events in our society. But they are also dramatic events and as such receive a great deal of media attention. Continued concern with their causes and prevention is both necessary and desirable. However, as happens with so many other types of crime, we must also strive to prevent our fear of its happening from growing in disproportion to its actual likelihood.

Be Careful,
Mr. President

I worry a bit more these days about the awful possibility that someone will assassinate our president. Of the eighty-three attempted and actual assassinations of high government officials in the United States since our country began, the targeted victims were one in every thousand congresspeople, one in every 142 senators, one out of every 116 governors, but one out of every 4 presidents. Only one cabinet member and one Supreme Court judge—no vice presidents—have been targeted. Clearly, there is a positive relationship between the importance of the office and the likelihood of an assassination attempt.

Analysis of the eighty-three attempted and actual assassinations reveals that most were motivated by real or perceived personal and sometimes political grievances and eleven of them are believed to come from organized crime. But all eight of the incidents involving presidents—except perhaps the attack on Harry S. Truman by Puerto Rican nationalists—appear to have been committed by mentally disturbed persons. Although the Secret Service has considerable sophisticated technology and knowledge of human behavior, the behavior of mentally disturbed individuals is quite difficult to predict.

True, we know that all seven of the presidential assassins were, in addition to their shared mental condition, White males, slender, loners from unhappy homes, having difficulty in relationships with women, suspicious of others, and harboring grievances that they perhaps tried to resolve by projecting the blame for their troubles on the most powerful figure in the nation. Unfortunately, such a profile is common, at least partly speculative, and provides little of use for prevention purposes. Potential assassins may display suspicious behavior in proximity to the president: unusual dress; shouting; reappearance in different locations; picketing, calling, letterwriting, or other reflections of ideological intensity; unusual interest in the intended victim and/or prior assassinations.

However, an unknown number of such persons has always been with us. Why is it that my concern about assassination is heightened now? Researchers have carefully examined when during America's 220-year history the assassinations that were attempted or carried out and what was going on in the country at those times. It is clear from this work that their occurrence is not random, nor is it something that occurs after any given number of years. Instead, attempts on the president's life in the United States seem to take place at times when (1) there is much challenge to and weakening of our shared democratic values, (2) the media are full of hate messages, defamation, and even vilification of the president's policies and personality, (3) many groups exist that directly promote an ideology and tactics of violence, and (4) persons with a propensity to commit violence exist and come forward. I fear I have just described much of what is occurring in the United States today. Assassination requires an assassin. But assassins emerge from the conditions of their day.

Still other research gives me pause and raises my level of concern. I refer to those studies of leader assassination in other countries and comparisons of these countries to the United States. Of eighty-four countries studied, we are fifth in frequency of assassinations. Most occur in Middle Eastern nations, Latin America, and Asia, but for the six countries in the world with populations of more than one hundred million, we rank first. The prime conditions for assassinations to occur in these other countries are during times of civil strife; political violence; a dissatisfied, frustrated populace; a significant level of tension among the country's minority groups; and a high homicide rate. At least a few of these conditions are accurate descriptions of the United States today.

So be careful, Mr. President. It may be a good time to be even more protected and prudent than usual.

Training the Torturer

the use of torture is widespread in the world today, as it has been for centuries. One reasonable estimate is that it is part of state policy and practice in about half of the countries that make up the United Nations. This decision to use a variety of physical and psychological means to inflict pain and suffering in order to carry out repressive policies is typically made by a high-level administrator, be it the country's president, the region's governor, or the city's chief of police. However, the president, the governor, and the police chief almost never are the persons actually administering the beatings, the electric shock, the near-drownings. Someone much lower in government rank does the dirty work.

Who are the world's torturers, and how did they get that way? Are they, as many falsely believe, sadistic monsters sought out in order to capitalize on their already existing enjoyment of cruelty? Or are they, as in fact has been repeatedly shown, merely ordinary men, trained first by the events and pressures of their time and place and then by deliberate and systematic indoctrination, to perform acts of brutality that others and even they themselves had never imagined they could do?

Research in several countries has compared in detail the backgrounds and personalities of persons who have committed sustained acts of torture to the backgrounds and personalities of regular citizens. In each of these studies, results indicated that torturers and non-torturers are essentially similar. Family background; school, work, or criminal history; various personality traits; mental health—all show no significant differences. These several investigations, then, lead to a frightening conclusion. The world's torturers are, at root, simply ordinary people committing extraordinarily atrocious acts.

The training of torturers occurs along two paths. One is simply living in a society in which political and economic conditions develop that facilitate the use of torture. The second is direct and systematic indoctrination of the potential torturer into the beliefs and skills that make up this cruel craft. National conditions favoring the acceptance and widespread use of torture are several. Torture and torturers are most likely to develop and flourish in societies with serious social, political, or economic problems that seem difficult to control; popular ideologies that promise a better life and that blame a particular subgroup of the population for the failure of progress toward that life; the tendency to devalue and scapegoat that subgroup; an emphasis on what psychologists call "just-world thinking" in which people are believed to get what they deserve (so, those being tortured must deserve what they are getting); a strong belief in the cultural superiority of one's own group or nation as compared to others; and a widely held tradition of respect for and obedience to authority.

Given an environment such as this, fertile for the development and acceptance of torture, how are those selected to carry it out to be trained? The methods often used are the same training procedures widely used to teach other types of skills: modeling, which involves expert demonstration of the skills by more advanced persons; graduated tasks difficulty, requiring learning the skill in steps of escalating difficulty; and generous use of rewards and punishments in response, respectively, to correct and incorrect skill performance. Algebra, driving an automobile, and knitting a sweater are learned by these means, and so too are the techniques of torture.

Professor Janice Gibson at the University of Pittsburgh describes this learning process employed in training torturers who were soldiers in the Nazi military.

> When trainees were promoted to interrogation units, they were first assigned the task of guard in detention rooms, where they watched other servicemen torture. [They] were initially brought into contact with political prisoners when they carried food to the cells. Eventually they were required to give the prisoners some blows, and then to participate with other servicemen in group beatings of prisoners. Finally, they were required to carry out individual tortures.

If they did well at this task, rewards followed: loosened military rules, leaves of absence, free rides on buses or meals at taverns, enhanced bonding with other servicemen in their group, and promises of job placement when military service was over. Punishments for failure or resistance to perform as required included intimidation and threats to both the serviceman and his family, including the threat of making the soldier take the prisoner's place. When this combination of effective training methods was used, as it was, on trainees kept in isolation from all but their new colleagues in the torture business, and indoctrinated to believe they were joining an elite military in-group with its important and special contribution to the larger society, the training outcome was almost inevitable: A new torturer was born.

We suggested earlier that the world's torturers are ordinary people inflicting extraordinary pain. It is also clear that such ordinary people can be systematically trained to do so by very ordinary and widely used training methods.

Female Aggression

because males throughout the world commit so many of the acts of aggression that occur, not a great deal has been written about aggression by females. However, the little research on this topic that has been done reveals some interesting information.

Compared to males, women and girls tend to be more empathic and therefore less likely to be aggressive in the first place. When they are, again compared to males, they are more likely to attack weaker targets, such as elderly parents, younger siblings, or their own children. They feel more guilt and anxiety about their behavior and are more likely to expect retaliation by the victim. Women are also substantially less likely than men to be aggressive in front of other people (besides the target person). Men seem to find more satisfaction in acting up in front of an audience.

There seems to be some evidence and much speculation suggesting that the level of aggression by females has risen considerably in recent years. Some have wondered if such a change is connected to the greater freedom and equality women have begun to receive in other aspects of their lives. As is true for males, a great deal of female aggression occurs during adolescence.

A quarter of the juveniles arrested in the United States each year are girls. Thus, the ratio of boys to girls arrested is four to one (nine to one for violent crimes). This means that about 350,000 girls are arrested each year.

Out of the total juvenile arrests for violent crimes, 8 percent were girls in 1965, 11 percent were girls in 1975, and by 1989 the figure had risen to 12 percent. Yes, the level of aggression by females seem to be creeping upward.

Still, it should be emphasized that crimes by males are by far the more serious problem. Boys far outdistance girls not only in the number of crimes but also in their seriousness. Boys start earlier on this path, continue longer, and are much more likely to extend their criminality into adulthood.

Research on how boys and girls grow up shows that there is much more pressure on girls to conform to moral behavior, much more disapproval from others when they do behave in an aggressive or delinquent manner, and substantially fewer opportunities to actually engage in criminal behavior.

Maybe it is for these reasons that, when they do commit crimes, their crimes—much more so than for boys—are the nonviolent crimes of shoplifting, running away, and prostitution.

Approximately one million children are runaways at any given time in America, and another million "throwaways," more or less told to leave. Half of these two million children are girls, many of them often forced by circumstances to survive by street crimes.

So the pattern for aggression by females in the United States seems to be slowly changing, unfortunately, not for the better. Too bad; males commit so much violence that there is all the more need for females to be models for all of us of nonviolent rather than violent behavior.

Will He or Won't He?

citizens try to do it when they learn
that someone who just completed a prison term for rape is moving into
their neighborhood. Abused wives try to do it. Parole boards try to do it.
Judges and mental health experts try also. But no one does it very well.
Accurately predicting whether or not someone will behave violently is
very difficult. When citizens, judges, parole boards, psychiatrists, or my
fellow psychologists try to do it, they are wrong at least half the time!

Their incorrect forecasting is of two types. False positive predictions
estimate that the person will behave aggressively at some later time, but
he or she does not. False negative predictions occur when the prediction
is that the person will not act aggressively, and he or she does.

Why are correct predictions of violence so difficult to make?

Even a person who is aggressive quite often is still not aggressive most
of the time. So one reason such behavior is hard to predict is that it
doesn't happen very frequently.

A second reason for the difficulty concerns how the prediction usually is made. Predictions of future violence are almost always based only on
qualities of the person whose behavior is being predicted. How often was
the person violent in the past, and how long ago? What is the person's age,
sex, education, employment history, attitude, personality? If he or she is a
prison inmate up for parole consideration, add the predictor of how well
or how poorly he or she behaved in prison.

Trying to predict violence in this manner fails so often because it doesn't take into account two important causes of violence: where the person will be and with whom he or she is likely to be interacting. Will he or she be living in or spending much time in a neighborhood with a high crime rate, low police or pedestrian surveillance, many bars, transients hanging out, and several tempting crime targets? Each of these qualities of the person's environment leads to a more likely prediction of future violence.

With whom will the person be interacting? Violent behavior is almost always at least a two-person event, and frequently the behavior of the eventual victim helps make the violence occur.

Two men are sitting in a bar. One insults the other, pokes him hard with his finger, calls him stupid and worse, and asks the other man if he'd like to make something of it. The second man takes out a knife and stabs his provoker. To the police, the stabber is the perpetrator, but the victim certainly shares at least some of the responsibility for his own victimization. Therefore, predicting violence will be more successful if qualities of the person's family, peers, co-workers, and others he or she is likely to associate with are taken into account.

Drugs and alcohol are also important in trying to successfully predict aggression. Is the person whose future behavior we wish to estimate likely to have access to and actually use such substances? Likely to become violent when under their influence? Likely to commit crimes to obtain money to buy drugs or alcohol? Likely to spend a lot of time in high-violence settings in order to obtain drugs and alcohol?

Even if we get better at forecasting violent behavior, what shall we do with such information? Fortunately, we still live in a country in which persons are punished for crimes they actually commit, not those they might do. We presume innocence; we reject preventive detention or selective incapacitation. This is as it should be.

Yet if we become better able to predict aggression before it happens, abuse can be reduced, and lives may be saved. It is important that those responsible for this difficult predictive task work hard at increasing its accuracy but also work equally hard in making sure the information is put to humane and constructive use once it is obtained.

Corporate Violence:
Aggression in Denial

Our murderers, muggers, rapists, and abusers are front-, back-, and middle-page news in America's newspapers every day and fill our television screens as well. But more deadly, more damaging, and more hurtful to many of our citizens is a type of violence much less discussed, much less frequently published in our papers: aggression by the modern corporation.

Take your pick, the list is long: inadequately tested drugs; unsafe foods; toxic chemical dumps; poisoned drinking supplies; cover-up of the effects of breathing coal dust, cotton dust, or asbestos fibers; defective contraceptive devices; implanted medical equipment turned harmful after implantation; automobiles that catch fire or explode on impact; and much more.

Corporate employees as well as consumers of their products are at risk. There were 2.2 million disabling work injuries and thirteen thousand deaths in a recent year in the United States from work-related accidents. Our citizens who purchase and use what our corporations are selling sustain approximately twenty million product-associated serious injuries each year. Of these, one hundred thousand cause permanent disability, and thirty thousand result in death.

If anywhere near such victimization figures were the result of street crimes by individuals, our prisons would perhaps be jammed with twice the million and a half persons incarcerated now. No, instead of arrest, prosecution, and incarceration for criminal behavior, such corporate violence is dealt with, at its most punitive, by cease and desist orders, warnings from regulatory agencies, hotly contested product recalls, government-financed pollution cleanups, minuscule fines, and out-of-court settlements with no admission of guilt or responsibility.

More frequently, it is not dealt with at all. As Professor Stuart Hills of St. Lawrence University put it, "Biases favoring large corporations are so deeply ingrained in the American culture and political structure that . . . we simply do not see corporate crime as crime."

Such a "see no evil, especially by ourselves" bias is most certainly also true for a great many corporations themselves. It is a bias expressed in several ways:

■ **Displacement of responsibility.** Corporate violence may be described by management as "an act of God," "a force of nature," "a technical error," or, in an especially egregious twist, as the fault of this or that regulatory agency for their enforcement of unfair and restrictive laws. Worse still, the victim may be held responsible for his or her own victimization. The rash of automobile crashes, the industry claims, stems from irresponsible drivers and not product defect. The contraceptive device, when it malfunctions, is not from anything wrong with the device; the problem, it is held, grows from improper insertion or the sexual promiscuity of the user!

■ **Denial of responsibility.** All corporations are organizationally arranged in a hierarchy, from line worker at the bottom to C.E.O. at the top, with many managerial and labor positions in between. Each person in this hierarchy has his or her own, often specialized, task contributing to the company's final products. In such a highly segmented context, with each person doing his or her own often small part and motivated to keep the job as well as move up the corporate hierarchy, it often becomes easy to close one's eyes and mind to the fact that ultimate injury to others has been made more likely. Some have called this a kind of "ethical numbness."

■ **Denial of injury.** Displacement and denial of responsibility for dangerous products and practices may lead to the serious injury or death of workers or consumers, but at least under both of these circumstances the corporate employee can claim no deliberate intent to injure. Actual denial of injury, however, seems to me to involve greater culpability. Falsifying laboratory tests, taking serious safety shortcuts, or refusing to recall products with known defects certainly ought to be considered fraudulent, criminal acts.

How may corporate violence be reduced in a society correctly described by professor Hall as "a capitalistic economy dominated by multinational corporations where the profit motive is supreme, where decentralized decision-making diffuses responsibility, where the quest for economic success and security are managerial imperatives"?

Building on Professor Hill's suggestions, we believe the answer lies in the meting out of serious punishments for violations and serious rewards for regulatory compliance. Punishments possible but rarely if ever employed include heavy fines, both of the corporation and its officers as individuals; jail time for serious offenders; requiring convicted corporations to advertise their crimes; appointing public interest representatives to corporate boards; encouraging and protecting whistle-blowers; and even, as an ultimate punishment, capital punishment of the corporation by revoking its corporate charter.

In a highly competitive society, one perpetually keeping its eye on the bottom line (corporate profits), rewards for *not* cutting corners or falsifying test results may be harder to come by. Yet the use of punishment alone as a way of seeking to change individual or company behavior is not enough. Perhaps especially in the present era of strong attack on government regulatory agencies, efforts to change corporate behavior will work best when they also include a serious effort to "catch them being good."

How to concretely turn responsible, nonviolent corporate behavior into bottom-line assets, beyond such intangibles as goodwill, public recognition, and a positive corporate image, is not readily apparent. Successful attempts at doing so, however, are likely to be well worth the effort.

Victims

Targets of Aggression:
Who Is Vulnerable?

Remembering the Victim

a violent crime takes place, and immediately the personnel, energies, and funds of a host of agencies—police, district attorney, the courts—are mobilized to apprehend, detain, and convict the perpetrator. Are comparable resources mobilized to deal with the needs of the victim? Until recent decades, the answer was no, but matters have changed considerably.

Beginning in the 1960s and growing steadily since then, victim/witness assistance programs have been established in almost all American states. From twenty-three such programs in 1975, there now exist six hundred, serving more than a million victims each year. Yet there are six million crime victims in America annually, suffering financial and property loss and often physical and emotional injury as well.

Many of the victims of crime, especially violent crime, cannot afford the expense of seeking compensation for their loss or injury via civil action against the perpetrator. Even if they could, the perpetrator may not have been caught; or, if apprehended, and the victim sued successfully for damage and restitution, the perpetrator may also be a low-income or unemployed person with few or no resources.

So sources other than the perpetrator must be sought if the financial loss of the victim is to be even partly compensated. Such financial assistance is one of the several services that victim/witness assistance programs try to provide. Though certainly short of fully adequate funding, both federal and state compensation legislation and federal crime fines and penalties have at least provided such monies for a portion of violent and other crime victims.

In most states, the persons eligible for such compensation are:

- The innocent victims of compensable violent crime

- Good Samaritans injured while attempting to aid victims or police

- Dependents of innocent victims or Good Samaritans who are killed as a result of the crime

Victim/witness assistance began primarily as a resource for those persons injured by domestic violence: battered women, abused children. Rape victims, too, received early and continuing attention by these programs. In recent years, victims of yet other violent crimes have been serviced.

In addition to aid in seeking or actually providing financial assistance, these programs typically are excellent referral sources for needed crisis intervention, counseling, or physical needs (food, shelter, clothing, transportation, or medical). Crime victims are usually also the major witnesses to the crime, and thus these programs also seek to provide needed assistance in dealing with the courts.

Program staff typically will make an effort to explain to the victim/witness the way the court works; provide court escort, including not only transportation but also moral support; and intervene with the person's employer so that testifying doesn't cause further loss or problems.

The fact that only one out of six crime victims seeks any of these services is probably the result of several factors, but chief among them is that most people do not know they exist. If you or anyone you know is the victim of a crime, call your local district attorney's office. There is a very good chance there will be a victim/witness assistance program right in your own community.

A Personal Note
on Being Mugged

most of my recent professional work concerns juvenile delinquency: Why does it happen and what can be done about it? The approaches we have developed to deal with such youngsters have received fairly widespread use across the United States and beyond. Some years ago, the Ministry of Justice in Warsaw invited me to come to Poland to share with them information about this work.

It had not been long since the demise of communism in Poland and Eastern Europe. One of the several consequences of this change was a major reduction in the power and credibility of all government agencies there, including the police. Knowing about this and about the resulting substantial recent increase in crime, I made a mental note before my departure from America to be especially prudent in where I went, when, and how, once I arrived in Poland. My first few days in Warsaw were eventful: nice people; good meetings. On the fifth day, suitcase in hand, my two traveling companions and I went to the main train station around 8 P.M. for a train to our next stop, the city of Lublin.

Knowing that public transportation locations were a favored crime spot, I looked around suspiciously as one of my colleagues purchased our tickets. One burly fellow was standing to the side, watching the slowly moving ticket lines carefully. At one point our eyes met and I gave him (no doubt my big mistake) my very best New York City look of cool indifference.

Many European trains have long, narrow passages between the train's inner wall and the compartment in which the passengers sit. A few minutes after getting our tickets, I entered the train and began, still with suitcase in hand, to struggle down our car's passage past other passengers to our compartment.

It all began and ended in what seemed like a flash. Two of the "passengers" coming toward me grabbed me and pinned me to the compartment's outer wall. Two others—one of whom was the man I had stared at by the ticket counter—came from behind and began searching through my pockets. In seconds, they had found my wallet, spoken to each other in Polish, and taken off. Out of the train, out of the station, out into the night.

A hurried and harried conference with the train's conductor yielded the fact that such events were more or less a regular occurrence these days. A later meeting with the eventually located Polish police was no more productive.

As the months and years have passed since this unpleasant experience took place, I have in a funny way come to almost treasure it. Before it happened, my work with juvenile delinquents and their victims grew from whatever I've learned from books, academic courses, talks with such youngsters and their victims, and similar formal educational experiences. The night I was mugged I stayed up all night. That night, and for many days afterwards, I felt the full welter of emotions common to so many crime victims—anxiety, shame, rage, guilt, self-blame, vulnerability, flashbacks—all of which I had earlier known about only in a removed, academic way.

I am prudent in my own behavior, in ways I hope will prevent me from being mugged or becoming any other type of crime victim again. I would not have asked to be mugged in Poland, but I sure did learn a lot from the experience.

Gay-Bashing:
The Growing Crime

Norway and Sweden, it is almost totally acceptable. In Iran and Saudi Arabia, you may be put to death for it. America can't make up its mind.

In some parts of the United States, engaging in homosexual behavior is a private matter, not a public affront, and the gay or lesbian persons involved are left to live their lives as they wish.

Far too often, however, gay men and lesbians are treated poorly by their fellow citizens—with bias, with hostility, and at times with vicious, violent behavior. Gay bashing, unfortunately, is a frequent and growing American crime.

■ In 1984, in Bangor, Maine, three teenagers yelling "Faggot!" and "Queer!" assaulted a gay man and threw him over a bridge into a river where he drowned.

■ In 1988, a lone assailant stalked and shot two lesbians hiking in the hills of Pennsylvania, killing one of the women and critically wounding the other.

■ In 1994, in San Francisco, four men forced their way into a gay club. They physically assaulted three men, and yelled "Faggots!" as they left. One man had a broken nose, another required nine stitches, and the other received substantial bruises on his head.

Thousands of such hate crimes toward homosexuals occur each year in America. Twenty-four separate studies have documented that an alarming number of gay men and lesbians have been threatened (44 percent), been chased or followed (25 percent), had an object thrown at them (25 percent), been vandalized (19 percent), been assaulted (17 percent), been spat at (13 percent), or been assaulted with a weapon (9 percent). Out of fear of reprisal or police inaction, as many as five out of every six such crimes aren't even reported. Most other forms of hate violence, such as those based on race or religion, take the less physically violent form of graffiti or hate literature; only a minority are attempted or actual assaults. For gay men and lesbians, however, such physical assaults are substantially more frequent.

The consequences for the victim include physical injury (or death, seventy documented in 1994), depression, anxiety, withdrawal, and the sense of vulnerability and loss of self-esteem that other assault victims also experience. For gay men and lesbians, however, the consequences are greater. As others become aware they were attacked because of their actual or perceived sexual orientation, they may lose their job, be evicted from their housing, or be denied access to public services. Their partners and the gay community at large also suffer in response.

Who are its perpetrators? Most frequently they are small groups of White males, usually adolescents or young adults, especially for attacks on the street, in bars, at school, and on college campuses. In the American workplace, older adults are the most common hate criminals.

Regardless of the age of the perpetrators, gay-bashers typically are persons who have had very little contact with gay or lesbian individuals, who early in life were taught biased attitudes about people called *queers*, and who associate regularly with others holding prejudices like their own. They attack their victims, almost always strangers to them, as an expression of these prejudices, in a distorted effort to reaffirm their "manliness" and to gain status in the eyes of their fellow attackers.

What's to be done? All forms of bias and prejudice are easier to play out when we don't know "them" and who they are as real people. We imagine a stereotype and act against it rather than the actual person. Research teaches us that under certain conditions, positive contact between people who have stereotyped each other earlier can lead them to feeling better about each other. When previously biased persons learn that a friend, relative, or workmate whom they already know and like is gay, the biased people often shift away from biased attitudes. When asked, most people will say they don't know anyone who is gay or lesbian. But this is rarely true. If one out of every ten Americans is gay or lesbian, you can bet that your neighbor, your boss, your son or daughter, or your car mechanic is also.

So challenge that antigay joke the next time you hear one. Support educational efforts that teach kids just how human lesbians and gay men are. To help learn the very same lesson, seek to increase your own contact with gay individuals. You might even take a gay person to dinner. To change gay bashing from a growing crime to one that is shrinking in frequency, many more of us must find such ways to be part of the solution, not the problem.

Granny-Bashing:
The Quiet Crime

happens as many as two million times in the United States every year, but we rarely hear about it. Child and spouse abuse rightly receive a great deal of both media and medical attention, but physical or psychological assaults upon aged parents or other elderly citizens are spoken of infrequently and are much quieter crimes.

In 1995 in America, average life expectancy is seventy-two years for males, seventy-nine for females. We are living longer, and most of us are living well. But one in every fifty of our fellow citizens aged sixty-five to seventy-two, and one in every fifteen over seventy-three years of age, are persons in need of long-term care for physical or mental impairments.

It is these elderly individuals (most frequently aged females) who often are most vulnerable to being abused. They are frail. Their needs may place heavy demands on others, often their own children, especially their daughters. Many of these daughters hold full-time jobs, have few siblings of their own with whom to share caregiving responsibilities, and, in addition to caring for their mothers, must at the same time care for their spouses and children.

Such caretaking stresses take place in a very youth-centered society, one that frequently discriminates against and devalues its aged citizens.

Most caretakers, in fact, do take care of their aged parents with consistent love, support, and responsibility. For some, however, the burdens are too great, and their stress levels find expression in repeated and serious abuse.

The abuse may be physical: hitting, pinching, pushing, physical restraint, or other forms of bodily harm. In addition, or instead, the abuse may be psychological. The elderly person is threatened, intimidated, humiliated, cursed at, or worse. Or, in what has been termed *material abuse*, the person's financial resources are exploited, manipulated, or just plain stolen. A final form of granny-bashing is neglect. The person is ignored for many hours, social contact is restricted, food or prescribed medicines may be withheld.

As with younger targets of abuse, the elderly victim suffers not only the immediate injury itself but such consequences as increased depression, anxiety, sleeplessness, and eating difficulties. Not uncommonly, the aged victim blames herself or himself for the abuse, feels both guilty and intimidated, and thus says nothing about it.

The perpetrator, too, reports nothing of course and will usually deny her or his abusiveness if confronted. Thus the crime remains a quiet one, its continuation undeterred by discovery.

Elderly abuse happens. Although rough estimates of its incidence are available, much less is known about why it happens, or what to do to prevent it, than is the case for child or spouse abuse. In 1995, 13 percent of the population of the United States was sixty-five or older; that figure will grow to 18 percent by the year 2040. If all goes well, each of us will be aged someday. For their sakes, for your own sake, we need both more information and some insistent shouting about this quiet crime.

People and Animals:
A Love-Hate Relationship

human aggression toward animals is not a subject of much scientific study. Human to human or animal to animal, yes, but not cruelty to animals by people, even though both in the past and today there seems to be a great deal of such aggression.

The bull-baiting, cat-skinning, cock-fighting aggression-for-entertainment of past eras has been largely replaced by more modern forms of cruelty to animals. One recent study, for example, reported in detail on the practices employed over a ten-year period in animal slaughtering plants of the United States and other countries. One-third of the slaughterhouses tolerated deliberate, repeated acts of cruelty.

One especially interesting finding from this research was that the countries (Holland, Sweden) and country regions (north rather than south) in which the handling of animals on their route from life to human food was most humane and least aggressive are also the same countries and regions with the lowest levels of human-to-human aggression.

Of course, we do not treat animals only with cruelty. The other side of our love-hate relationship with them is one of kindness. Through the centuries, although cruelty to animals always existed—albeit in ever-changing form—we have also been kind and even affectionate toward animals. From biblical injunction to legal protection codes—and because of the importance of animals in early industry, agriculture, warfare, and as pets—we also often care well for, and care deeply about, our animals.

True, we kill them by the millions, some by accident, some in scientific research, some for "sport," but mostly as food. Nevertheless, we are ambivalent about how they fit into our lives.

One researcher has speculated that an important factor in how we feel about and treat animals is how similar we think they are to humans. Perhaps, he suggests, if we believe they think and feel pain, fear, anger, and affection and therefore are more like us, we are less able to hurt them. If they are different from us in such ways, on the other hand, cruelty is more possible. Such "us" versus "them" perception underlies much human-to-human aggression; why not human-to-animal also?

What about those people who do hurt animals? Are they also likely to be more aggressive to other people? Some studies have found just such a relationship. In one of those investigations, for example, it was found that 25 percent of aggressive (adult) criminals had abused animals five or more times when they were children, whereas only 6 percent of nonaggressive criminals had, and none of the noncriminals. Other research has shown higher rates of animal abuse by parents who also abuse or neglect their children. In fact, in one study of fifty-seven homes with pets in which there had been child abuse or neglect, 88 percent of the animals had also been abused.

What would motivate such behavior? Actual attacks on humans by animals are very rare, so aggression toward animals is almost never a matter of self-protection. One interview survey revealed the following motivations:

- *To control behavior,* the most common example being as punishment when a pet disobeys, soils, etc.

- *To retaliate* for a particular behavior by the animal, the goal being revenge, not the use of punishment to teach.

- *To retaliate* for a particular behavior by another person. Here, the animal may be owned by the target person (for example, the rabbit in the movie *Fatal Attraction*) or may serve as a revenge symbol (for example, the dismembered horse's head found in the intended victim's bed in *The Godfather*).

- *To express prejudice* against a particular species. For some reason, over the centuries, cats have been a favorite target of such human aggression.

- *To express more general, free-floating hostility*, literally using the animal as a scapegoat.

- *To enhance one's own reputation* for aggressiveness or toughness, motivation that may underlie such events as bullfighting, bronco-busting, and steer wrestling.

- *To displace the target of aggression* from another person (who might retaliate) to a safer victim, an animal.

Folks gotta eat, and we're not all about to become vegetarians. So animals will continue to be raised and killed for human food. Folks like to stay healthy, so most of us will continue not to object to the necessary use of animals for medical research. And folks like to be entertained, so zoos and circuses with animal acts will continue to be with us too. But none of these major uses of animals need be places for their abuse.

To quote Professor Ronald Baenninger, psychologist at Temple University and the primary researcher in this field of aggressive behavior, "It is possible to put human needs first, while treating other species with the respect that they deserve."

Torture:
Aggression to Extreme

most nations that do it don't brag about it, so exact numbers are not known. One good recent estimate is that as many as 90 of the world's 214 countries today make use of systematic torture— the deliberate infliction of severe pain and suffering, both physical and mental.

The torture techniques that nation-states employ, many of which are literally thousands of years old, include:

■ **Active physical pain.** This most common of torture methods seems limited in awful variety only by the limits of human creativity. Techniques used include beatings with fists, clubs, whips, barbed wire, and other instruments; breaking limbs or eardrums; amputation or crushing of limbs or digits; blinding; pulling, or drilling healthy teeth; insertion of objects into bodily orifices; electric shocks to various parts of the body; burning; stabbing; and many other such methods.

■ **Passive infliction of pain.** These many techniques cause pain and suffering by passive means, such as being tied up, confined, or forced to remain in uncomfortable positions for long periods; the lengthy use of solitary confinement; extended exposure to sun, rain, cold; being tied up and suspended by hands or feet; and many more.

■ **Extreme exhaustion.** Forcing the prisoner to engage in strenuous physical activity to a point of total exhaustion. Heavy lifting, prolonged exercising, forced running are some of the primary methods of this type, often combined in actual use with sleep deprivation, inadequate diet, and beatings.

■ **Fear induction.** Fears of many types may be aroused—of mutilation, indefinite captivity, harm to family and friends, and one's own death. To instill this last fear and bring it to a point of terror, captors may bring the prisoner to a state of near drowning or suffocation, force the intake of enormous quantities of liquid, or administer drugs that inhibit breathing. Mock executions, forced participation in humiliating and revolting acts, being constantly hooded or blindfolded, deprivation of sanitary facilities, and unpredictable alterations of leniency and severity are additional methods of mental torture designed to induce fear.

These several procedures for administering the severe aggressions of torture are designed, according to Professor Peter Suedfeld of the University of British Columbia, to bring about a defeated and compliant state in the prisoner. Sought by the captor is prisoner *debility*, a state of exhaustion; *dependency*, the total belief that his or her fate is in the hands of the captors; *dread*, the intense and constant state of fear and anxiety; and *disorientation*, involving uncertainty, confusion, and a deep sense of being lost.

Given the vast catalog of torture methods available, it is no wonder that their prolonged and severe application to defenseless prisoners so often is successful in bringing about this state of debility, dependency, dread, and disorientation. For what purpose? What are, and have been, the goals of torturers since early Egyptian, Greek, and Roman times, in so many societies over the centuries and to the present time?

■ **Information.** To force the prisoner to provide factual criminal, military, or political information that he or she is believed to possess.

■ **Incrimination.** To force the torture victim to identify and implicate other persons suspected of participation in real or imagined activities held undesirable by the captors.

■ **Indoctrination.** To compel the prisoner to give up certain beliefs and, instead, adopt others more acceptable to the captors.

■ **Intimidation.** To arouse fear not only in the prisoner but in other persons as well. Here the goal includes but also goes beyond the prisoner himself or herself, as the torture is made public.

For those who survive extended or even brief periods of torture, the price may be heavy. Among the several consequences often reported by survivors, sometimes decades after their release from torture, are the stressful reexperiencing of the trauma while awake or asleep; a variety of physical symptoms—headaches, eating difficulties, sleeplessness, for example; a cutting off of feelings and even relationships, called *psychic numbing* or *emotional anesthesia*; memory losses; intense guilt; difficulty concentrating; depression; and bouts of deep anxiety.

The severity and length of such post-torture symptoms seems to be a combined result of the victim's age (children and the elderly do poorly), previously developed ability to manage stress effectively, intensity and length of the torture experience itself, and strength of ties to supportive persons and groups after release.

Torture is indeed aggression to extreme. From ancient to modern civilizations it has been with us, and the evidence of recent decades is that its use is not decreasing. Perhaps the best we can do is to continue to try to understand it, to publicize it, and to condemn it.

Victim Once, Victim Twice?

criminals

are not equal opportunity offenders who spread their criminal activities evenly around the community. Quite the contrary: Those who have already been crime victims are much more likely to be victimized again than are people who have never been targeted. In fact, the single best predictor of whether or not a person is likely to be a crime victim is whether or not he or she has been a victim before.

Only 1 or 2 percent of the general population are victims of violent crime, but 17 percent of these victims are victims again three times or more. In fact, this very small number of people account for 45 percent of all violent crime victimizations! At the other extreme of the crime continuum, the same revictimization facts are true. Only 1 percent of the population reports three or more car thefts, but this 1 percent accounts for 22 percent of all car thefts. Once a house is burglarized, the chance of a repeat burglarization is four times that of homes never burglarized. Thirty-eight percent of assaults, 37 percent of vandalism, 24 percent of burglaries, and 17 percent of robberies are revictimizations. It is indeed a frequent occurrence, accounting in some crime surveys for as much as 79 percent of all crimes reported.

Not only are crime victims likely to become victims again but also other people living in the same households as the victim are themselves more likely to be the targets of (often the same) crime than are people living in households in which no one has been victimized. Revictimization happens not only to people but to places also. Some locations, especially such businesses as bars, convenience stores, fast food restaurants, and gasoline service stations, are frequently targets of revictimization.

Another fact about repeat victimization is that, regardless of the type of crime involved, it often takes place very soon after the original crime. In one city, for example, the likelihood of a repeat burglary during the first month after a burglary took place was twelve times the city's general burglary rate, but after six months the chances were only two times the general rate. In another city, there were 296 property crimes in their thirty-three schools. Of the 263 of these crimes that were repeats, 208 occurred within one month of a previous victimization. Racial attacks, domestic violence, and various business crimes have also been shown to recur a short time after their first occurrence.

The two facts—that crime victims are frequently revictimized and that such repeat crimes often occur soon after the earlier crime—are pieces of information that can be put to good use for crime prevention. Some cities are already doing so. In one instance, within twenty-four hours after the occurrence of a home burglary, victims were supplied with a portable alarm system connected to their local police station. In another, small neighborhood watch groups, consisting of all of the neighbors in the immediately surrounding homes, were mobilized rapidly to keep an eye on homes that had been broken into.

Whatever prevention approach is used, it clearly makes sense to invest much of our crime-fighting energies and resources at those locations and at those times at which crimes are most likely to take place. In the meantime, if you are a crime victim, be wary; a repeat performance may be headed your way.

Places

Where Does Aggression Happen and Why There?

Hot Spots

the U.S. Office of Juvenile Justice has a category of young criminals that it uses in its work called *S.H.O. kids*, Serious Habitual Offenders. These are the juvenile delinquents who are multiple recidivists, committing crime after crime.

Less well known but perhaps equally important in trying to better understand and reduce repetitive crime is what might be called serious habitual places, or crime hot spots. These high crime frequency locations, once identified, can be better studied to learn about qualities of places associated with frequent crime and can be better protected to reduce such crime rates.

Where are these crime hot spots? Bars are one such location. In one large American city, for example, there were a total of 112,142 serious crimes on the city's 4,396 blocks over the two years that were studied. This averaged out to 25.5 crimes per block. But on the 499 blocks on which there was a bar, there were 21,099 such crimes, or an average of 42.3. Persons under the influence may be more likely to become perpetrators (of aggressive crimes) as well as victims (of such crimes as robbery or mugging).

In a second large city, slightly more than half of all police calls for which cars were dispatched were sent to only 3.3 percent of all possible locations. All of this city's 4,166 robbery calls were located at only 2.2 percent of all possible sites; all 3,908 auto thefts were at 2.7 percent of such sites; and all rapes at just 1.2 percent of all locations. Stated the other way around, 94 percent of all the city's locations were free of these crimes for the period studied. They were crime cold spots!

Let's look more closely at these serious habitual places. In the study just described, the top hot spots were a large discount store in a low-income neighborhood (810 police calls), a large department store (686 calls), and a corner with a bar and a convenience store (607 calls).

Across the country, convenience stores have been an especially frequent crime target, particularly those close to heavy auto traffic routes, thus assuring a good supply of potential offenders, and, increasing the chances that they will not be seen, those next to vacant lots or with few other stores or little activity nearby.

There have been successful efforts to turn this particular hot spot, convenience stores, into a less frequent crime target by increasing the chances that the criminal will be observed by others. Such efforts include selling gas and enlarging the store's parking lot to bring more people to the scene, thus providing more observers to scare off criminals. Other tactics: improving store lighting, moving the cash register to the middle of the store, removing vision-blocking signs from the store windows, and staffing the store with two clerks rather than one.

Other crime hot spots? City areas within one block of public high schools or rapid transit stations; arcades and food fairs in shopping malls and apartment houses near malls with such features; public housing enclaves; and, the hottest spot of all, the crack house. This last location is such a source of violent crime that in some cities, in addition to arresting its criminal occupants, the house itself has been sentenced to capital punishment, as one criminologist put it, and destroyed!

Reducing crime requires better understanding of criminals, of why they perpetrate and how. But crime occurs in particular places, some more than others. Let's study people, but let's study places as well.

Rapist, Where Are You From?

rape is committed by a rapist, who is responsible for his behavior. But whether or not a rape occurs appears to be a result of many factors, some of which concern certain qualities of the state or region in which the rapist lives.

Professor Lawrence Baren, a sociologist at Yale University, and his colleagues tested the idea that the frequency of rape in different parts of the United States was associated with the amount of legal violence in each area studied. Their prediction was of a kind of "cultural spillover" from legal to illegal violence.

They measured legal violence in two ways. First, for each state, they came up with a score (the Legitimate Violence Index) combining the state's level of:

■ *Mass media violence*, as shown by the readership rate of violent magazines and by the audience level for the six most violent shows on network TV

■ *Government use of violence*, as indicated by state legislation permitting corporal punishment in school, rate of prisoners receiving the death sentence, and rate of actual executions for homicide offenses

■ *Participation levels in legal violent activities*, as reflected in the number of hunting licenses per one hundred thousand population, the state of origin of college football players, National Guard enrollment,

National Guard expenditures, and lynchings during the period 1882–1927

Their second measure for estimating each state's noncriminal violence level (the Violence Approval Index) was based on national surveys, directly asking people about their beliefs concerning when physical force was or was not appropriate. Scores for each of the fifty states and the District of Columbia were tabulated according to the following types:

■ *Government policy:* the percent of people in the state who support greater military spending, support the death penalty, and oppose gun permits

■ *Punching a stranger:* the percent of people in the state who approve of punching an adult male stranger under certain circumstances, for example, if he hits a woman, or hits your child, or if he is a drunk who bumps into you or your wife

■ *Police punching a citizen:* the percent of people in the state who approve of a police officer punching an adult male citizen under certain circumstances, for example, if the male is saying obscene things to the police, or attempting to escape, or is a murder suspect

Their research results were clear. The more that aggression is treated as a legitimate or legal behavior in a state, or the more a state's citizens approve of noncriminal aggression, the more rape that state has. Legal violence does spill over to illegal violence.

Other findings from this research tell us still more about where rape is likely to happen and the qualities of those locations. Six of the top ten rape rate states are in the American West; the country's lowest rape rates are in the north central and northeastern states. In the years in which this recent research was done, the highest rape rate locations were, in order, the District of Columbia, Nevada, Alaska, California, and Florida. The lowest rates in increasing order of frequency were North Dakota, South Dakota, Maine, Iowa, and Wisconsin.

States with high rates of rape compared to those with low rates, in addition to mere expression of and belief in legal violence, also contain a greater percent of divorced males and a greater proportion of men between the violence-prone ages of eighteen and twenty-four.

A good way to sum up this research and its significance is to quote from the researchers:

> The findings suggest that if rape is to be reduced, attention must be paid to the abundance of socially approved violence, not just to criminal violence. . . . This will be a formidable task, considering that economic and racial inequality, corporal punishment of children, violent sports, mass-media violence, capital punishment, and other forms of legitimate violence are woven into the fabric of American culture.

What's Happening
at the Frat House?

charter, on paper, in yearbooks, the American college or university fraternity is an organization devoted to brotherhood, service, and recreation. In reality, far too often, among the primary activities of the four hundred thousand current fraternity members are injurious hazing of pledges, serious destruction of property, sexual abuse of female party guests, and, at its worst, gang rapes.

Who are these young men, and what is there about fraternity life that promotes this streak of nasty violence?

With no doubt a great many exceptions, fraternity members are often young men with a particularly narrow view of, and preoccupation with, masculinity. Their concerns are with competition, dominance, material possessions, athletics, drinking, and, especially, sexual prowess with women.

Applicants not sharing or showing these preoccupations are often not accepted as pledges or drop out along the way, thus leaving the membership to become a highly masculinized brotherhood. Once formed of such individuals, the norms of the fraternity—the shared attitudes held by the members—and the process of living together combine to actively encourage violence as a frequent means of expression.

In many fraternities, these norms consist of a sense of superiority, loyalty, secrecy, group protection, and, most directly relevant to sexual abuse and rape, the view that women are objects or commodities to be manipulated and exploited.

The manipulation of women into unwanted sexual encounters often occurs, as one researcher put it, through the use of alcohol as a weapon. Getting females drunk to achieve sexual compliance is a not infrequent fraternity practice. Sexual ("notch-in-the-belt") contests, so-called pig contests (having sex with the woman the group considers least attractive), date report competitions mocking sexual encounters with women, and fraternity logs and newsletters with obscene humor are other common ways of demeaning women and thus making it easier, because they are inferior, objects, less than "us," to perpetuate violence against them.

In addition to this sense of the superiority of one's own group and the stereotyped view of women, a process psychologists call *groupthink* further promotes the likelihood of violence. Groupthink is the tendency in groups for attitudes to converge, for disagreements to fade, and for there to be continuing pressures to "think as one."

Thus we have in the fraternity a tight, loyal, often secretive collective of males, who are preoccupied with their own and their group's masculinity and who strongly agree in regarding women as objects to manipulate and sexually exploit. Add to the mixture the lowering of inhibition and resistance via excessive alcohol consumption, and the stage is well set for serious acts of sexual abuse.

Numbers are hard to come by in this context, but reports of violent or sexually violent behaviors by individual or groups of fraternity men— toward property, pledges, other fraternities or, especially, women—are far from rare. One authority estimated that more than 90 percent of the gang rapes that occur on college campuses are perpetuated by fraternity men.

Sexual behavior in young people is normal and healthy but only when occurring in the context of commitment, mutual consent, and affection. When it occurs under duress and as a result of deliberate manipulation and exploitation, it is not sex but aggression that is taking place. It is not behavior to be expected and welcomed but instead to be brought out into the open and condemned.

Worry in the Workplace:
From Harassment to Homicide

all is not well in the American workplace. Violence has come to both the convenience store and corporate headquarters. Four percent of all murders in the United States takes place in work settings. In a recent year, 1,063 persons died in this manner. Most were robbery victims, but 149 of these homicides were to settle imagined or real grievances or had other nonrobbery motives. In addition to murder, violence at work finds expression in 16 percent of all the assaults in America, 8 percent of the rapes, and 7 percent of the robberies.

This is not all. Hate crimes and terrorism too have appeared at the workplace, as the World Trade Center bombing in New York City and the bombing of the Federal Building in Oklahoma City sadly illustrate. In all, there were 110,000 incidents of workplace violence in a recent year, varying from harassment and threats to homicides and bombings and costing American industry an estimated 4.2 billion dollars.

This huge figure reflects the multiple costs wrought by violent episodes: employee replacement and retraining, management diversion for investigation and training, increased insurance and security, property damage, medical and post-trauma stress treatment, decreased productivity, litigation, and more. Violence in the workplace is a costly event indeed.

Perhaps we ought not be surprised at its arrival at the job scene. After all, what goes on at work merely reflects what is occurring in the community at large. As our homes, streets, schools, and media grow in violence, so too will our work sites.

To be sure, violence in the American workplace is not a new phenomenon. Industrial sabotage, as one example, was not uncommon as far back as the earliest years of the industrial revolution, at least to the 1820s. But its levels of frequency and severity seem worse.

Analyses of workplace violence reveal three types of causes: frustrated employees, sick organizations, and a weakened general economy. The reasons why a worker may grow increasingly dissatisfied, disturbed, and prone to violent acts are many and varied: unmet needs and job expectations, work overload, job insecurity, stagnating or declining income, skills and knowledge that are ignored or underused, perceived injustice or insults, irritating co-workers or supervisors, reprimands, negative performance reviews, oversupervision or monitoring, or simply getting fired.

This litany of poor working conditions can be made worse, can become more likely to result in employee violence when the general nature of the company is itself dysfunctional—understaffed, overly rigid and authoritarian, chronically involved in labor-management disputes, excessively demanding of and generally unresponsive to its employees.

The situation grows still more volatile when our country's economic picture is bleak and fewer alternatives are open to angry employees seeking better arrangements. In the 1960s and 1970s, more than 80 percent of workers losing their jobs were able to find new employment at comparable wages. By the late 1980s, the number able to do so had shrunk to 25 percent and today is even less. From 1987 to 1992, 9.7 million workers in the United States lost their jobs. One-third of these persons remain unemployed, and many of the two-thirds who did succeed in finding new jobs in fact found only temporary or part-time employment, often with little job security or benefits.

Thus we see that a wide collection of negative qualities of the job, the company, and the economy may come together to yield levels of employee frustration and anger that increasingly culminate in violent behavior. What is an employer to do?

A good beginning starts with who is hired in the first place. Violence is a difficult behavior to predict. Personal stress or disturbances and alcohol or drug problems may make it more likely, but the single best predictor of future violent behavior is instances of such behavior in the past. Watch out for the job applicant with a history of frequent disputes, threatening actions, harassment, and the like.

Once hired, a good violence-management rule is to catch it low to prevent it high. Even though chronically angry people are hard to approach, best to have at it in its milder forms and not let it grow. When the disputes, threats, and harassment that you tried to screen for actually appear, that is the time for action. Waiting for fights, assaults, or other high levels of violence to occur before acting is a serious management or supervisory error.

But what kinds of actions? I believe our corporate system in the United States—not unlike our common childrearing practices, our public school systems, and other systems—relies far too heavily on punishment techniques to alter or control employee behavior and far too little on creating everyday work conditions in which violence by employees becomes an unlikely alternative. Thus, instead of heaviest reliance on enhanced use of security personnel, police, surveillance, threats, reprimands, docking, suspension, and firing, we urge creative use of decision centers, participatory management teams, employee wellness programs, employee assistance programs, flexible work schedules, family support programs, enhanced workplace safety, employers who come out from behind their roles and titles, fair and bias-free employment practices, peer review panels, nonauthoritarian worker supervision, constructive grievance processes, mental health counseling, and, when necessary, effective and humane outplacement procedures.

I would certainly expect that the employee who feels respected as an individual and treated like an adult is far less likely, even in hard economic times, to behave violently.

Aggression Around the World:
Any Lessons for America?

yes, because of widespread and rapid communication around the world, we all are truly becoming one global village. Trends and fashions in food, clothing, entertainment, and lifestyles—as well as in crime and violence—spread at times almost instantly via satellite-relayed television images and computer networks.

But cultural, national, and regional differences still persist. Therefore it continues to be interesting, and maybe even valuable in the possible lessons it holds for America, to ask, How do they do aggression elsewhere, and how is it dealt with?

In Sweden, it is against the law for parents to spank their own children.

In Iran and Saudi Arabia, thieves may still be punished by having their hands cut off; adulterers may be stoned to death.

In western New Guinea, the Kapauku tribe punishes homicides that take place in their own or immediately surrounding villages but not those that take place outside this "home" location.

In Japan, police are community service focused and are the center of each neighborhood's communication network. New residents check in with them, and they make a how-is-it-going visit to each home at least yearly.

In Canada, contrary to myth, the mounties don't always get their man. But they come close, with a crime clearance rate among the best in the world.

There are a number of so-called primitive groups scattered across the world, whose members rarely show aggression, criminal or otherwise. They include the Tasaday of the Philippines, the Punan of Borneo, the Hadza of Tanzania, the Bihor of Southern India, the Australian aborigines, the Yamis of Orchid Island off Taiwan, and the Hopi, Zuni, and the Papago Native Americans.

In the People's Republic of China, the death penalty, not unlike its earlier use in the United States and numerous other nations, is a public event. Members of the perpetrator's community gather at the designated site to witness the execution, usually done by shooting the individual in the head.

In Germany, as in a great many other countries, it is the rate of violent juvenile crime in particular that has increased, including homicide, rape, assault, and robbery.

In Finland, the suicide rate is one of the highest in the world, and its level of homicides is also well above that of a great many other countries. Although such high levels of aggression toward self and others grows from many causes, Finnish scientists have in particular pointed to the high levels of alcohol consumption in their country.

In France, there has been considerable debate about the legitimacy and limits of self-defense (auto-defense) in which an armed citizen shoots an intruder (or a relative by mistake) in his or her home or business. In most such incidents, the victim has proven to be not an adult criminal but an adolescent.

In Holland, which has much shorter prison sentences than most countries for those who commit violent crimes, there is also one of the lowest violent crime rates in the world.

In Afghanistan, among the Taliban Islamic group, it is common practice for the father of murder victims to serve as the executioner of the crime's perpetrator.

In India, whose combined movie production is the largest in the world (Japan is second, the United States third), violent movies are common and quite popular among Indian viewers.

In Belgium, the youngsters who are most alienated from school and most bored with its curriculum, and who have the poorest relationship with their teachers, commit the greatest number of juvenile crimes.

In Israel, as has been found to be true in the United States, the rates of violent crimes decreased during times of war and increased in the periods following each war.

In New Zealand, the police are unarmed. Although this policy is slowly changing in parts of Great Britain, not so in New Zealand. Guns are rarely used by criminals in the relatively small number of murders that occur there.

In Nigeria, the punishment for committing an armed robbery is usually execution by lynching.

In Italy, as has been found to be true at different times in France, Great Britain, the United States, and elsewhere, there is more violent crime in the southern regions of the country than in the northern.

In Peru, as perhaps everywhere, one scientist attributed rising levels of violence to similarly rising levels of unemployment, underemployment, poor housing, inadequate diet, and overpopulation pressures.

In Turkey, especially its more rural and recently migrated urban areas, honor crimes and blood feuds are not infrequent. Common also in other Mediterranean countries, these are violent (often homicidal) acts designed to maintain social standing and respect (honor crimes) or exact revenge for perceived offenses to kin (blood feuds).

In Brazil's largest cities, a great many homes are surrounded by tall fences or walls, topped with sharpened iron bars. Few people venture out during the day wearing expensive clothing or jewelry for fear of becoming kidnap victims. Fewer still venture out at all at night. Those that do, by car, may slow down but only infrequently stop at red lights, fearing a robbery or carjacking attempt. Many feel they are, as one resident put it, prisoners in their own homes. However, Brazil also has police stations staffed entirely by women police officers, for female citizens to seek out if battered, assaulted, or raped.

In Sao Paulo, a resident psychologist insisted on including the category "traffic violence" in his report on Brazilian aggression, indicating that aggressive driving habits there resulted, in a recent year, in eight times as many traffic deaths as in New York City and seventeen times as many as in Tokyo.

Any lessons for America here?

5.

criminal justice, criminal injustice

The Criminal Justice System

From Police Arrest to Parole Release

Police Stress

it had been a tough week for Officers Carl Bemstrem and Samuel Brown, though not very different from most weeks. They spent most of Monday in court waiting to testify about an arrest they had made a few weeks earlier but were never called to the stand. Tuesday morning they found out that another officer in the department, a friend of Carl's, had put his revolver in his mouth Sunday evening and blown his brains out. That was the third suicide of a fellow officer in Carl's precinct since he got there. Nothing happened Wednesday, just a boring, empty, routine day. Carl's stomach bothered him a lot that day, and he made a mental note to see the department's physician. All hell broke loose on Thursday. There was a big fire in a downtown lumberyard when they came on duty at 4 P.M., and Carl and Samuel helped redirect traffic. Then there was a really tricky domestic dispute call around 6 P.M. Samuel was a bit surprised over this one because most of the family fights in this neighborhood came on the weekends. He came within two inches of getting hit in the head by a flying ashtray. No counseling or arbitration on this call. They arrested the husband. The officers were wolfing down a quick, late supper around 8:35 when the Tempo service station robbery call came in. Because they knew that the perpetrator was armed and dangerous, the twenty minutes between the call and their arrest of George Harris seemed like two full days. Then, when they signed in on Friday, there were no congratulations for the Harris arrest; instead there was Supplementary Regulations

Bulletin 714A, spelling out in no uncertain terms that officers of the 44th precinct had recently been too casual in the care and wearing of their uniforms and that such sloppiness was to cease immediately. The worst part of the day for them—the worst part of *any* day for the police officer—came on Friday afternoon. Two bodies were discovered in a shed in the lumberyard that had burned the day before, and Carl and Samuel were assigned the death notification responsibility for one of the deceased. As they drove to the address, Samuel kept imagining what the victim's wife might say when he told her . . .

As this fictional yet very real job description reveals, the daily demands placed upon a great many of America's 550,000 police officers are stressful indeed. The job is complex and unpredictable. Diversity of roles that constitute a police officer's work include being on-the-spot judge, counselor, peacemaker, service provider, and physical protector. There is shift work, social isolation, physical danger, managing aggressive individuals or groups, negative public image, family and marital conflict, departmental overregulation and restrictions on behavior, inactivity and boredom punctuated with hyperactivity and job overload, red tape, pay inequities, court rulings and scheduling as well as perceived court leniency for perpetrators, and more. It would be difficult to come up with other occupations that are so broadly, diversely, and continuously stressful.

In the short run, stress can help the person become alert and mobilized and thus deal more effectively with his or her environment. However, continued stress has clearly negative effects. This is precisely the outcome for many American police officers. Compared to the general population, as well as to almost any other profession, police rates are higher for alcoholism, divorce, suicide, depression, and a wide variety of stress-related physical problems, such as headaches, ulcers, and hypertension. Psychologists have helped develop and evaluate several apparently effective treatment methods for this broad variety of stress reactions, including cognitive stress inoculation, biofeedback, progressive relaxation, systematic desensitization, autogenics, and visualization.

Maybe we as citizens can help too. Police work is tough work. Next time we see a cop, perhaps we can smile and give silent thanks.

The Lineup

having witnesses to a crime view possible perpetrators in a lineup (or in mug shots) is a common procedure used by police departments across the United States. The testimony of such witnesses has been the target of considerable psychological research. One group of researchers describes the ideal eyewitness as an individual who (a) saw all that happened during the crime, (b) accurately placed these perceptions (encoded them) into memory, (c) stored the encoded perceptions in memory, and (d) fully and accurately retrieved the encoding from memory in the form of later reports. Unfortunately, this ideal is rarely even approximated because substantial inaccuracies may occur at each stage of the memory process: encoding, storage, and retrieval.

When witnessing a crime or other event, the person's ability to encode what he or she sees or hears is influenced by several factors. Eyewitness testimony research has shown that the more frequently something is seen or heard, the longer it is seen or heard, the more organized or meaningful the event, and the more serious the apparent crime being perpetrated, the greater the accuracy of eyewitness identification. What is encoded? In a study of one hundred street crimes, eyewitnesses reported, in order of frequency, the perpetrator's sex, age, height, build, race, weight, complexion, hair color, and eye color.

Witness expectations, stereotypes, cultural biases, and prior information about the crime also influence what is perceived and encoded. Thus, a great many factors associated with either the event or the witness can negatively affect the accuracy of information encoding. The same is true for the next stage of the memory process, storage.

Some of psychology's oldest research findings are directly relevant to the storage component of memory and to accuracy of identification in the police lineup in particular. In 1885, memory researchers demonstrated the existence of a forgetting curve, in which considerable information is forgotten shortly after an event, followed by the more gradual loss of additional information as more time passes. Thus, the longer the storage period, the more one forgets.

New information learned after the event during the storage period also actively and negatively influences the storage process. With regard to the police lineup, for example, innocent persons (not at the crime) whose pictures happen to be included in the mug-shot books looked over by the witness after the crime but before the lineup are more likely to be incorrectly identified as the perpetrator of the crime.

As was true for encoding and storage, there are several sources of possible inaccuracy when the witness seeks to retrieve and report his or her recollection of the crime. The specific retrieval questions asked, for example, may be a cause of distortion. Unbiased instructions to the witness at a police lineup, "The perpetrator might be in this lineup" as compared to biased instructions, "The perpetrator is in this lineup," led to a greater number of both accurate identifications when the perpetrator was in fact present and accurate rejections when he or she was not present.

Who besides the possible perpetrator actually appears in the lineup will also influence retrieval accuracy. The more people who appear in the lineup are similar to the perpetrator in at least some important, observable way, the lower the accuracy. On the other hand, if all the other people in the lineup (the *foils*) are very different in appearance than the suspect (in gender, race, position, behavior), such bias will likely lead to greater chances that the suspect will be misidentified. Many eyewitnesses appear to approach a police lineup with a "culprit-present assumption" (he's in there), and they then proceed to finger whichever person is closest to their recollection. Some authorities have suggested that one good way to counter or at least reduce such lineup bias is to first have the witness view a *blank lineup* (all foils, no suspect included) before using a second lineup that includes the suspect. If the witness identifies a member of the blank lineup as the criminal, the bias has been revealed and can be taken into account.

Multiple retrievals is a further source of retrieval inaccuracy. Retelling a description of a crime or reidentifying an alleged perpetrator leads to clearer and clearer statements and more and more certainty and confidence in one's (perhaps incorrect) identification with each retelling.

Interestingly, the relationship between eyewitness certainty and accuracy of identification is weak in study after study. If witnesses' stress level was high during the crime, if their exposure to the criminal was brief, if the criminal was of a different race, and if a weapon was involved—all of these decrease identification accuracy. But don't expect the jury to believe all this. There is a 73 percent conviction rate in trials in which evidence against the defendant was eyewitness testimony!

So at each stage of the memory process—encoding, storage, and retrieval—there are common sources of inaccuracy associated with the event itself, the passage of time, competing information, and the witness himself or herself. It should not surprise us, therefore, to learn that in the several studies examining eyewitness accuracy, the percentage of correct identifications in lineups was always less than 50 percent and frequently less than 20 percent!

Jury Selection

a central component of the American legal system is the representative jury. In theory and partially also in fact, the typical American jury reflects the nature and diversity of the community in which the trial occurs. The usual first step in selecting a jury (called the *venire* or *to come when called*) is to constitute a pool of potential jurors from voter registration lists. Because citizens who are young, poor, or minorities are underrepresented on such lists, the degree to which the juror pool selected actually represents the community is thus reduced.

Once selected from the voter registration list, potential jurors are each sent a jury questionnaire by the jury commission. The pool is further reduced at this point—based on questionnaire responses—by the disqualification of those who cannot read, cannot speak the language, are employed in criminal justice occupations, or have criminal records. Those for whom jury duty might function as an undue hardship, on themselves or their clients, may be exempted from the pool, namely, physicians and nurses. Once the juror pool is constituted in this manner, the next stage in juror selection is the *voir dire*, that is, the choosing of the actual jury.

The voir dire, in operation, is a questioning of potential jurors by either the prosecution or the defense. Up to a set number, either attorney may excuse any given panel member on a peremptory basis (no explanation needed) or for cause (because of clear juror bias, for example). Thus, the purported goal of the voir dire is to select a fair and unbiased jury.

In reality, it has been shown that in the typical voir dire, only 20 percent of the usual half hour devoted to each panelist is spent on questions designed to identify trial-relevant biases. Eighty percent of the voir dire looks like the trial has already begun! The attorneys conducting the voir dire spend most of their time seeking to indoctrinate the panelist, commenting on points of law, ingratiating themselves, forewarning jurors about given items of evidence, and engaging in similar behaviors. For these reasons, as well as because of its considerable cost in time and money, in some jurisdictions the amount of attorney questioning is limited by the court, or, more drastically, the voir dire is conducted by the judge himself or herself.

How well does the voir dire system work, whether conducted by attorneys or judges? Prevailing opinion (there is little actual evidence) concludes that it probably eliminates the openly prejudiced and sensitizes those selected to try to set aside their prejudices when deliberating.

The American legal system proceeds on an adversarial basis, in which two opposing sides actively seek to convince a jury that their version of the truth is more accurate. It is in this adversarial context that there began in 1968 one of psychology's most controversial contributions to legal process, systematic or scientific jury selection.

Systematic jury selection is the use of psychological techniques to obtain a final jury likely to be most favorable to one's own side and least favorable to the opposition. This is the identical goal already sought by attorneys preparing for trial, but the means utilized are different. Instead of the attorney's usual unsystematic interview of voir dire panelists, the psychologist conducting a systematic jury selection may use

- Surveys of the community in which the trial is to take place in order to identify characteristics of persons who favor one's own side as well as the opposition, so that voir dire panelists with the same or similar qualities favoring one's own side can be accepted.

- Information networks, that is, sources in the community who know and are willing to describe the actual jury panel members. (Attorneys or their representatives may not contact panel members directly, as this would constitute jury tampering).

- Juror ratings, in which the psychologist observes the voir dire, draws "clinical impression–like" conclusions based upon panelist answers and nonverbal behavior and advises the attorney for whom he or she is consulting accordingly.

- Small group research findings to draw conclusions about how a given panelist may behave and vote in the context of the particular jury being selected, namely, how responsive he or she may be to the status of others, likely alliances among particular panelists, resistance to conformity pressure, and so forth.

Adequate research examining the effectiveness of systematic jury selection has yet to be conducted. The anecdotal evidence examining its effectiveness appears to be largely positive, beginning with its first uses in the 1968 trial of Black Panther Huey Newton and the 1972 trial of the Berrigan brothers and employed as recently as the trial of O. J. Simpson. In reality, it has been used infrequently, probably in part because of expense.

Some legal figures strongly object to its use, fearing in effect the buying of a biased jury. Others welcome such consultation and view it as merely one more component in an adversarial system designed to do the best job for the client. What do you think? Should the courtroom door be locked when the psychologist tries to enter, or is such assistance in jury selection fitting and proper?

Witness Testimony

many psychologists have studied witness testimony in considerable detail and have much to offer both the student of courtroom behavior as well as the practicing attorney. A crucial aspect of witness behavior is witness credibility. It has been shown that witnesses are more believable when they speak with a conversational delivery, few nonfluencies, moderate to slightly rapid speaking rate, lower pitch, a variety of intonation, eye contact, moderate use of gestures, and a somewhat extroverted style.

Witnesses not only influence others, such as the jury, as a result of such qualities as their credibility but they in turn are open to influence. During the trial, for example, the examining (or cross-examining) attorney's questions may cause distortions in what the witness remembers. This influence has been called *destructive updating*. One researcher, for example, showed that incidental mention in the attorney's question of such in fact absent details about a crime as a "stop sign" or "passing the barn" increased the degree to which witnesses mentioned a stop sign or barn in later testimony. In a related demonstration of question-induced bias, it was shown that the intensity of the descriptive term used by the questioner when inquiring about a speeding accident directly influenced the witnesses' average estimates of the vehicle's speed, namely "smashed" (40.8 m.p.h.), "collided" (39.3 m.p.h.), "bumped" (38.1 m.p.h.), "hit" (34 m.p.h.), and "contacted" (31.8 m.p.h.).

In addition to such destructive updating, witness testimony may be influenced in the direction of identification and other errors by additional types of distortions. *Illusory recollections* occur when the witness includes in his or her description of the crime event information actually a part of something that took place either before or after the event itself. *Unconscious transference* is a form of witness misidentification in which the witness identifies as the criminal a person who actually was an innocent bystander he or she has seen before, either in person or in a mug-book photo. The more similar the bystander is to the actual perpetrator, the more likely the misidentification. Another witness distortion is *verbal overshadowing*. Research has shown that witnesses who first attempt to create an Identi-Kit rendition of the perpetrator don't do as well in identifying the actual perpetrator accurately compared to those not trying to construct the perpetrator face in this way, possibly because erroneous images or memories from the Identi-Kit session intrude on later attempts at perpetrator identification.

What about the witness whose testimony is in error not because of faulty memory or examiner questioning bias but because of deliberate deception? Four major areas of deception detection have been explored: the polygraph or lie detector, hypnosis, voice indicators, and nonverbal cues.

The polygraph is a device composed of three (or more) instruments designed to record on a moving paper chart changes in skin conductance of electrical currents (the galvanometer), respiration (the pneumograph), and blood volume and pulse rate (the cardiophysmograph).

Two forms of examiner questioning are most common in current use of the polygraph. In the *control question technique*, the examiner asks not only questions about the alleged crime or event but also other (control) questions designed to elicit guilt or anxiety in the subject. If the subject is telling the truth, users of this approach claim, then polygraph response to control questions should be greater than response to event questions; if lying, then the opposite should be the result.

In the *guilty knowledge technique*, the subject is asked questions about the crime whose answers could be known only to the perpetrator. The subject's responses to such questions are then compared to responses to diverse control questions. In several investigations, polygraph accuracy—especially its skin conductance component—has been shown to be between 70 and 90 percent correct. On the other hand, there are a series of countermeasures that some subjects have used successfully to deceive the polygraph and its operator. These include such techniques as mental distraction; dissociation from the questioning by doing a monotonous task; posing and answering one's own questions during the exam; thinking erotic, embarrassing, or painful thoughts; flexing various muscles; and taking depressant drugs.

Critics of polygraph use point out that the high levels of accuracy reported in polygraph evaluation research reflect its use at its best, not its typical employment with often less experienced examiners. False alarm rates under these latter circumstances, it is suggested, are considerably higher than the reported 10 to 20 percent.

Hypnosis has been employed in legal contexts in a number of different ways. One is *hypnotic screening* during the voir dire in order to detect panelist prejudice or bias. A second is to help determine the *mental state* of an accused individual at the time of an alleged crime. Hypnosis has also been used to help prepare the *anxious witness* with posthypnotic relaxation suggestion. Finally, in its most common legal usage, hypnosis has been employed to *improve the process of remembering*. However, research evaluating the success of hypnosis-aided remembering has not been supportive. What has been shown is that under hypnosis, witnesses are more suggestible and show a greater tendency to agree with the interrogator. Because of these findings, there is a growing trend for courts to reject hypnosis-aided testimony.

What about voice cues? As a rough guide to deception detection via vocal cues, it has been shown that many individuals, when lying, will show (a) reticence, reflected in fewer total words and shorter statements than when they are telling the truth; (b) vagueness, as shown by a restricted verbal code, that is, fewer *different* words, fewer facts, broader generalities; and (c) negative emotion, that is, more disparaging remarks and fewer group references.

An attempt to make much more specific and exact use of voice qualities for detecting lying has emerged in recent years in the form of voice prints. These are oscillographic representations of spoken sounds that supposedly identify unique elements of an individual's vocalizations. Neither the legal profession nor the psychological research community has yet accepted the validity of this approach. Research shows voice detection by this means to be no better than chance in identifying deception.

Although there is some research showing that hand and foot movement may prove to be especially good nonverbal sources of information about intentional deception, because most people studied concentrate on changing their facial expressions, most nonverbal deception research to date has focussed on signs of lying on the face. Deceivers have been shown to try to change their facial expressions in four different ways as part of their effort to falsify.

They may change the *pattern* of their expressions: For example, the shape of the mouth or cast of the eyes may not fit what is being said. The *timing* of their expressions may also be a good leakage clue of deception, or how long it takes for a given expression to appear in a particular context, how long it remains on the face, and how long it takes to disappear. The *location* or occurrences of a given expression in relation to an ongoing conversation may be a third leakage of deception clue. Finally, persons who are trying to deceive by "putting on" a false facial expression sometimes reveal their true feelings in very brief *microexpressions*, which may occur just before, during, or just after the deceptive expression.

We have seen then that witness testimony may be biased by what and how attorney questions are asked or by deliberate deception. Aside from polygraph evidence (which is not admissible in most courts), neither hypnosis, voice prints, nor the use of nonverbal cues are yet up to the task of reliably detecting such deception. Given these realities, plus the fact that witness memory may itself be faulty in the first place, there is considerable reason to be skeptical of much witness testimony in American courts.

Jury Deliberation

consider the jury and how it reaches its decisions. Key aspects of this process include its size, the decision rules it must follow, how it deliberates in the jury room, qualities of the person on trial, and juror bias.

Although only about 8 percent of all criminal cases are decided by a jury, in the United States about three thousand different courts (criminal and civil) use approximately twenty million juror-days each year. Six percent of the general population will be called for jury duty at some time in their lives. Although American juries have consisted of twelve jurors since the jury system began in the nineteenth century, in recent years some jurisdictions have been experimenting with the use of alternative sizes, particularly with juries of six.

In experimental studies of the effects of jury size, small juries (six people) as compared to large ones (twelve people) allowed more participation for each individual, had fewer women or minorities, and in general examined the evidence presented less carefully. The large juries provide more skills and knowledge, have potential for being a more representative cross-section of the community, and provide more opportunity for a viable minority opinion (but also a powerful majority opinion) to emerge. It has been estimated that small and large juries would disagree in their verdicts about 14 percent of the time.

It is not only size of jury that recently has become the focus of experimentation but also their decision rule. In the traditional decision format, the unanimous jury, all must agree for a decision to be reached. In quorum decision formats, some proportion of the members of the jury less than unanimity are necessary for a verdict.

Research has shown that quorum juries, as compared to juries needing unanimity for a verdict, show better recall of arguments and higher levels of communication among members but often stop deliberating when they reach the required majority. Thus, the quorum jury provides less opportunity than does the jury requiring unanimity for dissenters to have their say. Although unanimous juries are more likely to become hung, they do nevertheless allow for greater presentation and examination of minority viewpoints.

What about jury communication patterns? Research has shown that the individual selected by the jury at the outset of its deliberations to serve as foreperson is more likely to be male than female, have prior experience as a juror, be of higher occupational status, and be seated at either end of the jury's rectangular table. Behaviorally, the typical foreperson usually assumes a moderator role, concerned with maintaining rules of procedure and facilitating the jury's deliberation rather than advocating a particular point of view.

Seating position is associated not only with foreperson selection but also apparently with the behavior of the other jurors as well. Those seated at either end participate most actively in the jury's discussion; those seated at the table's corners tend to be least active. Higher juror levels of occupational status and education are also associated with higher rates of participation. There is no apparent relationship between level of participation and juror age, but jurors under thirty tend to be more lenient in the verdicts they support than those over thirty.

During the jury's deliberations, the communication flow is such that early in the process most jurors direct their comments toward the jury as a whole or to those in apparent agreement with them. As the deliberation progresses and opposing factions become clearer, jurors increasingly direct statements toward members who disagree with them. The actual content of what is discussed is diverse. According to one study, the breakdown in the typical jury is juror opinions on facts of the case (29 percent), comments on the process of deliberation (26 percent), personal experiences (22 percent), references to testimony (15 percent), and references to the judge's instructions (8 percent).

Content of statements, of course, varies from juror to juror. Less well-educated jurors appear to devote more of their comments to the testimony, personal experiences, and their opinions; better educated jurors will focus more in a relative sense on jury procedures and the judge's instructions. Juries will also often discuss testimony or other matters that have been explicitly prohibited by the judge's charge to them. They also have often been shown to discuss, although it is not a part of their responsibility, the consequences for the defendant of a guilty verdict (the verdict of course is a jury matter but sentencing, in most jurisdictions, is a prerogative of the court).

Jury research has also focussed on defendant characteristics. Though studies show that it is clearly *evidence* that looms largest in the typical juror's decision making, jurors also tend to be responsive to a variety of defendant characteristics. Defendant *gender* is one such influential quality relevant to the verdict reached. Men are five times more likely than women, for example, to be convicted of spouse murder. In laboratory research on juror behavior, conviction for grand larceny results in shorter sentences for women offenders than for men.

The defendant's *physical attractiveness* is a second outcome-relevant characteristic. Less attractive defendants tend to receive longer sentences, at least in experimental studies of courtroom decision making. Physically attractive defendants are more likely to be acquitted, unless their attractiveness was used as a part of the crime, as in a swindle. Highly authoritarian jurors tend to be most influenced in their decision making by defendant attractiveness. Defendants whose victims are attractive receive harsher sentences, again in laboratory and not actual courtroom settings, than do those whose victims are unattractive. On both counts, defendant attractiveness and victim attractiveness, jurors are more influenced than are judges.

Defendant *race* is a third characteristic associated with juror decision making. In all too many American jurisdictions, African Americans are more likely to be convicted than are White defendants and are more likely to receive longer sentences. In addition, African-American defendants whose victims were White are treated more harshly by many jurors than are Blacks with Black victims.

Aspects of the crime itself also influence the juror. Was it committed alone? Presence of an accomplice leads to a more lenient juror response. Who did the planning? Defendants who play a central role in planning a crime receive longer sentences than do those who serve as accomplices. Is there more than one charge against the defendant? If the evidence is strong on one charge, jurors are less likely to convict on the second charge. Was there much suffering by the victim? The more the victim suffered, the longer the suggested sentence by the juror.

An especially important set of influences upon juror thinking and decision making is the defendant's *behavior during the trial*. The defendant is more likely to be found guilty if he or she appears in court in custody (e.g., jail clothing, in handcuffs); than on bail (e.g., civilian clothes, no handcuffs), if extenuating circumstances relevant to the crime are presented by the defendant rather than an impartial other person; if the defendant protests his or her innocence too extensively; or if he or she fails to appear remorseful about the criminal behavior.

What are the influences upon the jury's decision making? We have seen thus far that in addition to the (highly influential) trial evidence, there are several factors that help shape the jury's verdict. These include, as we have noted, the size of the jury, its decision rule (unanimous or quorum), its communication pattern, and such defendant characteristics as gender, attractiveness, race, and behavior at the time of both the crime and the trial.

There are still further influences on juror decisions. One is juror bias. It has been shown that, on the average, 25 percent of all jurors believe an accused person is guilty; otherwise he wouldn't be charged. Thirty-six percent believe the defendant is responsible for proving his or her innocence rather than that the state has to prove him or her guilty. Juror decisions are also influenced by knowledge of a prior record on the part of the defendant. Such knowledge increases juror belief that the evidence against the defendant is strong, decreases juror willingness to dismiss damaging evidence, and increases the likelihood of a guilty verdict.

Seventy-four percent of all juries deliberate for less than two hours. Thirty percent reach a unanimous decision on their first vote. In 90 percent of the instances, the final verdict favors the view held by the majority on the jury's first vote. Seldom, therefore, does a position held initially by a minority of the jury prevail. Ninety-five percent of all juries do reach a verdict. When it is reached, the judge will agree with the jury's decision about 75 percent of the time, with most disagreements occurring when the defendant is acquitted.

It is clear that jury decisions rest on a varied and sometimes surprising set of juror, jury, and defendant qualities. Given that this is the case, perhaps it is fair to say that it is also surprising that so many trials seem to end with what appear to be fair and relatively objective verdicts.

Parole

parole is the conditional release of inmates from prison back to the community after serving a portion of their sentence. As of 1996, there were approximately 650,000 juveniles and adults on parole in the United States, under the supervision of more than two thousand separate parole agencies. Most function under the jurisdiction of state departments of corrections. They usually start to review inmates after one-third of their sentence is served. If parole is granted, it is almost always under certain conditions and stipulations, mostly concerned with a stable home environment, potential employment, and likely risk to the community.

The number and reasonableness of such parole conditions vary greatly from one jurisdiction to another and may include obtaining and keeping a job; attending academic or vocational school; participating in drug or alcoholism counseling; attending church; reporting in daily; and not drinking, signing contracts, associating with former prisoners, moving one's residence, voting, or traveling out of state. The typical parolee in recent years received an average of thirteen such conditions.

The use of parole began in sixteenth century England with the granting of reprieves and stays of execution to criminals who were physically fit for employment overseas to work in the American colonies. A more graduated, transitional system of parole emerged in certain other European countries. Ireland, for example, moved prisoners stepwise from strict imprisonment to government labor (chain gangs) to individual labor to "tickets of leave" involving first a conditional and then a full pardon.

The first parole ("good time") law in the United States appeared in New York in 1817, with its first major implementation occurring at Elmira (New York) Reformatory in 1876. Sentences there were indeterminate, their length a function of good behavior, and post-release parole supervision heavily emphasized gainful employment. The use of parole spread across the United States and by 1929 was adopted by all states.

Some criminologists believe that parole became widespread not because its use facilitated rehabilitation or reduced recidivism but because it helped prison administrators (via good behavior increasing chance of parole) maintain a more peaceful and orderly prison environment. It also helped district attorneys plea bargain (longer sentences were more attractive to defendants if the possibility of earlier parole existed), and it helped the community in that it extended supervision and surveillance of ex-inmates once they return to their communities.

There are two major problems with the parole process, however: It is often unfair and ineffective *before* the inmate's release; and it is often unfair and ineffective *after* the inmate's release. The parole decision-making process prior to an inmate's release suffers, first of all, from all the difficulties also associated with its companion procedure, the indeterminate sentence. The parole decision may be highly arbitrary and capricious as a result of a changing and prejudicial decision-making process. To a substantial degree, it denies or diminishes the legal due process to which the inmate is entitled because the parole board, not a trial judge, actually determines the length of sentence.

An especially strong objection to the parole process has been raised on two counts: regarding the degree to which the parole board considers not only the inmate's past behavior (his or her crime and in-prison behavior) but also, many believe quite unfairly, what the inmate is or is not likely to do in the future. This latter basis for reaching a parole decision is held to be unjust not only because it is an example of preventative detention (holding someone in prison longer because of something they might do, rather than a crime they've actually committed) but also because psychological research consistently demonstrates great difficulty in accurately predicting a person's dangerousness. One researcher has concluded that even the most sophisticated prediction methods yield 60 to 70 percent false positives, that is, people said to be dangerous who prove not to be.

There are also serious problems associated with the parole process after an inmate's release to community supervision. The problems associated with this latter phase are several. Parole officers are poorly trained, poorly paid, and usually burdened with caseloads so large that only cursory supervision is possible. In supervising, they are typically caught in the conflicting roles of cop and counselor, mandated to carry out supervision helpful to the ex-inmate as well as surveillance helpful to the community.

Perhaps the most telling criticism of parole is the absence of evidence that it has had any beneficial effect on recidivism rates.

Clearly, there is a strong movement in the United States to abolish this process and institute determinate sentencing in which both a fixed length of sentence and a fixed reduction in sentence for good behavior is stipulated at the time of posttrial sentencing. My view is different. I feel parole to be a valuable legal process whose perhaps imminent demise is due more to its misuse or inadequate implementation than its inherent weaknesses.

I agree with those who urge that new life be breathed into the parole process. In new and better form, parole would be more decentralized, parole officers would do less one-to-one casework and invest more time and energy in identifying and mobilizing community resources of value to the parolee, and greater emphasis would be placed upon finding or developing jobs for ex-inmates. I also believe parole will work best when it is used as but one of many alternative means for dealing with offenders. Other alternatives include community services orders, day fines, monetary restitution, neighborhood justice arbitration, nonresidential and residential care centers, work release, graduated release, and such split sentences (a combination of incarceration and community supervision) as shock probation (ninety days of incarceration followed by probation), shock parole (six months of incarceration followed by parole eligibility), and weekend jail. The alternatives are many. Let's be creative and try them.

Prisons and Prisoners

What Really Goes On Behind Bars?

Going to Prison as *Punishment*, *Not* for *Punishment*

imagine it. You must leave your family, home, friends, job, neighborhood. You must give up all decision making in your personal life: when to get up, what to wear, when and what to eat, when to speak, when (and if) to make a phone call or write a letter, when to go to sleep. You must spend each and every routine and boring day, week after month after year, in a large, crowded, impersonal institution peopled by hundreds or thousands of others like yourself. You must, in a great many of these institutions, also spend countless hours day and night vigilantly managing your behavior—what you say or do, to whom, about what—in order to avoid being punched, stabbed, slashed, or killed. All this is what going to prison in America is like. Imagine it.

In a wiser and less mean-spirited era, convicted felons were sent to prison *as* punishment. The several, long-term deprivations of personal freedom just described were, in combination, the punishment.

Today, much of America is increasingly of a different, much harsher mind. In the view of many of our citizens, persons sent to prison go there *for* punishment. Inmates, they believe, should suffer privations well over and above those associated with imprisonment itself.

Thus, Alabama has brought back its chain gang fifty years after it was banished from America as inhumane. For six-month stretches at a time, twelve hours each day, five men linked together by eight-foot chains connected to their leg irons work on roads, break large rocks into small ones, endlessly. The sheriff of Phoenix County, Arizona, now puts his prisoners in sun-baked tents, prohibits smoking or television, and serves bologna sandwiches and Kool-Aid as standard menu fare. An Illinois prison banned sugar, honey, and other sweeteners; and several prisons have removed all weight-lifting equipment. A North Carolina correctional center is, because of severe overcrowding, seriously considering *hot bunking*, which requires inmates to sleep in the same bed in shifts. A Tennessee legislator has proposed a bill under which certain felonies, in addition to imprisonment and a fine, would earn the perpetrator five to fifteen lashes with a cane. Other state prison systems are opting for reduced family visiting, no free postage, no furloughs, charging fees for medical or other services or "rent" for cell occupancy, no vegetable gardens, or other punitive measures.

More widespread than these examples, and more damaging in the long run to both inmates and the outside community, many educational, vocational, counseling, and recreational opportunities are being broadly restricted or eliminated in several state prison systems across the United States.

The American prison population exceeds one and one-half million persons. "Three strikes" legislation, the widespread use of longer and more rigid sentencing guidelines, and exceedingly severe sentencing practices even for "minor" drug crimes mean that our prison population in the years ahead will grow larger, more crowded, and more violent.

In our nation's recent past, "correctional institutions" actually sought to correct, not just punish. Yes, rehabilitation often failed, but some of the time at least, correction worked, and law-abiding, productive lives were the result.

But today is different, a time for get-tough, just deserts, retributional prison policies. Today, we double punish: first by removal from society, then by harsh or even brutal treatment within prison walls.

Crime must indeed have consequences. "You do the crime, you do the time" is still a wise cliché. But if our prisons become increasingly inhumane and harsh, we risk creating ever more brutalized and brutal convicts who are bitter about society and all the more primed to wreak vengeance upon it when they are released.

National recidivism rates consistently show that at least two-thirds of persons who serve time for felonies they have committed will carry out new, serious crimes after they are released. There are many reasons for such high rates of return to crime, but surely much of what does and does not happen during the prison term itself helps create such a dismal criminal spiral.

We need to put correction back into our correctional institutions but not by continuing to increase their discomforts, severity, and inhumaneness. Instead, we must continue to use, evaluate, and improve the personal, educational, vocational, and recreational opportunities that we all need—prisoner and free citizen alike—to develop into law-abiding, contributing members of society.

Voices From Prison

I get a magazine of which I suspect most of you have never heard: *Prison Life*. It is written by, for, and about prisoners, about the one and a half million men and women now incarcerated in America. The articles, letters, stories, and features are angry, sad, biased, fair, informative, amusing, scary, and more. In their own ways, they tell us as much and perhaps more about the American prison system today than do the many parallel writings of our politicians, criminologists, and similar professionals. What follows, then, is a sample of these prisoner voices from prison.

> The conditions that create most crime are poverty, racism, ignorance, idleness, and oppression of the weak, the poor, and the free thinkers by powerful and intolerant control freaks. At any given time, the vast majority of people in prison are there for committing acts that are crimes only because they offend the ruling powers.

> One of the guards here . . . told me that California's version of the three strikes law is a good thing for the state. People are tired of having their property stolen, he said, and they're not going to take it anymore. I understand, I said, but did he think that Ed, one of the three-strike defendants in our unit, deserved life? He's in here for shoplifting, and now he's facing twenty-five years to life. That's more time than most murderers get. . . . The three strikes law does not deter criminals. Most of them have no idea that the petty crimes they

are committing can be considered strikes. They think strike crimes must be violent or very serious. Not so. Fresh meat still arrives daily.

In order to secure any form of privacy, I have to go through a series of elaborate maneuvers. One way is my old curtain-on-the-shoelace routine. Imagine three well-worn, paint-stained sheets hanging over a pair of old shoe strings stretched across the front on my cell. . . . It's the equivalent of a "Do Not Disturb" sign. However, some people can't read. It's especially true when I'm in a compromising position, such as when I'm sitting on the toilet.

As in the free world, in prison you are known by the company you keep. Guilt by association. The cardinal rule here is do not get involved with recognized gangs or with cliques known for trouble-making or illegal activity. Refuse favors from anyone you think might be gang affiliated. To accept a favor may obligate you . . . to some future recompense. If asked to join a gang, decline tactfully. . . . Laughing at or otherwise "dissing" their colors by offhandedly rejecting an offer can mark you as a target.

We take no joy from cold food on dirty trays served with a scowl by our fellow prisoners. We eat three meals a day because the trip to the mess hall breaks up the monotony and marks time. Time that crawls so slowly the day never really begins, never ends.

In one obvious respect, being incarcerated is a trip back to virginity. There isn't "any" available, and just like in high school, all the guys are spending inordinate amounts of energy talking and thinking about it. The body can be imprisoned, but the imagination can't. If you don't believe me, consider those long, lonely nights you spend on your bunk alone. Just you and the memory of her, wherever she may be, whatever she may look like. Now that's prison. Certainly, one of the very first acts of freedom I will indulge in will be finding a woman. But not just for sex. I may want to listen to a woman's voice, the slightly higher pitch than I'm used to here. I'll gobble up every word. For me, it'll be live music.

What the average citizen doesn't know is that it's the conditions at the facility that not only set off the uprising but determine what will happen during the riot. If the administration encourages a malicious informant system, there will be some enraged prisoners looking to settle scores with the snitch who added years to their bids. . . . If the living conditions aren't fit for animals, like at Attica, the prisoners will use the riot as a way to voice demands to state officials.

The white shirts and the administration stand by and watch as their officers have their "getback." Prisoners are humiliated, slammed around, and beaten. Some stay strong; most succumb. This all goes on while you're leg-chained and cuffed behind your back.

Prisoners exit the buses slowly and stand waiting. Guards order them onto all fours. Working in two-men teams, guards shackle prisoners together in groups of five. Many men wear two pairs of socks to avoid skin burns caused by leg irons rubbing against their flesh. The chain gang workers pick up rakes, garden shears, and bow saws from an open trailer. The long work day begins. The men spend hours hobbling around, tripping over the chains and each other as they remove trees and clear brush, clean up litter and pull weeds. As cars and semis speed by, drivers honk, yell, and howl at the chain gang prisoners.

What I learned is that being a convict means you can never give in, you can never let them break you. It's better to die standing up for your beliefs than to go out on your knees as a rat, a coward, and informant.

Some men at Marion have grown up here in the harshest hole ever constructed. Deprived for so long of a normal existence, our measure of self-worth is gauged by our capacity to endure whatever physical or psychological torture is thrust upon us. Men along the tiers boast of surviving brutal riots, of running gauntlets of club-wielding guards, of being starved and beaten. . . . It is both an indictment of society and a human tragedy that the state of imprisonment in America has been allowed to degenerate to this level.

I'm serving a fifteen year sentence and this is my first time in trouble. At first, my wife told me, "Don't worry, I'll be right here for you." Now things have changed. . . . I remember the day when I surrendered myself to the police. She cried for hours. While I was in jail waiting to go to prison, we talked on the phone two or three times a day. She wrote me letters telling me how much she loved me. . . . [Now] the letters have stopped coming. When I got my case back in court, I tried to call her but the number was not working.

Missed birthdays become missed graduations become lost marriages become unattended funerals. Our families grow away from us and all we can do is play cards, watch "Gilligan."

Between 10 and 10:30, the cop in the bubble signals to me that I have a visit. The walk to the visiting room is always filled with a strange mixture of happiness and dread as I wonder what frame of mind she'll be in, what frame of mind I will find myself in. I am also, after all these years, filled with a kind of giddy joy at seeing the woman I love.

I'm tired of hearing how women get all the privileges and easy treatment. . . . It's a flagrant lie. I've been fed rotten food crawling with worms. . . . I've been thrown in dry cells and had cavity probes. . . . I've been caged without daylight for an eight-month stretch. Women prisoners get fewer privileges than men prisoners because we passively accept whatever "they" dish out.

With nothing to look back on but failure and nothing to look forward to but more time, we're trapped in a vacuum of meaningless, never-ending now.

In the slice of reality where I reside—prison—where innocence is unknown, weaknesses deadly, tough guys a dime a dozen, poets are revered. It is not the cat burglar, the bank robber, or the paperhanger who occupies the top rung in convict hierarchy. Only visual artists rival wordsmiths when it comes to who is granted respect. . . . Prison poets wield the sword that pierces the tumor of apathy, contempt, and complacency in the minds of the still free. We are the voices—screaming, exulting, groaning, whispering—that you cannot still, here in the belly of the beast.

Warning. Very soon the above-named man will once again be in your midst—dehumanized, demoralized, and bitter. . . . In making your preparations to welcome him back in respectable society, you must make allowances for the crude environment in which he has suffered for the past years and months. . . . Therefore, show no alarm if he chooses to squat on the floor rather than sit in a chair, or continues to X out each day on the calendar, or slyly offers to loan the mailman a pack of cigarettes. . . . Don't correct him if he chooses to cut his meat with a spoon rather than a knife or asks where to empty his plate after dinner. Don't be surprised if he immediately goes to his room whenever a bell rings. . . . For the first few months, don't be alarmed if he swipes the toilet paper, hoards the sugar, or stashes a spoon under his bed. . . . Keep in mind that beneath his pale prison exterior beats a heart of gold.

What is justice? Is justice making people hate the world? People who can't wait for a chance to get revenge? The day I walk through the front gate into freedom, will I truly be free or will I be a walking time bomb ready to explode at the slightest incident?

The Data-Proof Decision

death penalty is now legal in thirty-eight states and the list is growing rapidly. Twenty years ago, most Americans opposed the death penalty; now a large majority support it. What are we hoping it will accomplish?

If retribution and revenge are its goals, the passage of death penalty legislation clearly makes sense. Perpetrators injected (most common), shocked (next most frequent), gassed, hung (options in three states), or shot by firing squad (option in Idaho and Utah) will never repeat their crimes.

If deterrence is the goal, relevant data show the death penalty to be a failure. Murder rate comparisons of (1) countries with versus countries without a death penalty, (2) states with versus states without a death penalty, (3) states before and after they enacted death penalties, and (4) comparisons involving other relevant geographic entities demonstrate no superiority in murder rate decline or level favoring death penalty venues. In fact, not infrequently murder rates are *lower* in locations and at times when *no* death penalty is in effect.

One is left wondering just what is driving currently popular pro-death penalty decisions. Fear? Frustration? Political reelectability? Certainly not the relevant deterrence data.

In reflecting upon whether or not they themselves could commit a murder, in addition to acknowledging the immorality of such an act, members of the general public may also wonder if they'd be deterred at the thought of being put to death by the state if caught and convicted.

However, the vast majority of actual murders are acts of passion and do not involve prior consideration and weighing of pros and cons, of likely success and possible penalties. For most murderers, the death penalty is not a deterrent, because in the heat of the act future implications and consequences are not considered.

Those murders that are premeditated, and in which there is a careful weighing by the perpetrator of the possible punishments involved, are frequently also unlikely to be deterred by the existence of a death penalty. Considerable research has shown that the career criminal—even in the face of repeated incarcerations—grossly overestimates the odds of getting away with his or her crimes.

Past capture, rather than deterring the perpetrator's next crime, is often seen as a "corrective lesson," which the perpetrator uses to "do better" the next time.

Although America's adult crime rates generally are *not* growing at the present time, their levels are nonetheless dismayingly high and demand thoughtful and effective government and citizen response. The success of such response will clearly be greater when relevant data concerning deterrence are fully considered rather than totally ignored or distorted.

Each year, for the past several years, approximately twenty-four thousand American citizens have been murdered. In about 70 percent of these homicides, the murderer was identified and arrested. Yet only approximately three thousand of them now await execution on our death rows. Who gets chosen and who receives a nonlethal sentence, even in states that do have a death penalty?

The majority of men and women who await execution (or who have been executed in the past) are African American or Hispanic. African Americans convicted of killing a White victim are much more likely to receive a death penalty than are White murderers of White victims. In fact, regardless of skin color, anyone killing White people is more likely to wind up on death row than is a murderer of African Americans. There is also evidence that more male murderers than females, and more poor people than middle-class people are likely to receive the death penalty.

So in addition to the fact that it does not appear to be a homicide deterrent, we must ask whether the way in which the death penalty is applied—which murderers get it and which ones do not—is also grossly unfair.

We are almost the only country in the Western world to still use the death penalty. Do other countries know something that we don't know?

The Technology of Execution

will confess it up front. I am opposed to capital punishment. However, since so many of my fellow American citizens these days feel otherwise, perhaps the history and a detailed description of the current technology of this process that they favor would be useful.

The first recorded legal execution in what was to become the United States took place in the Colony of Virginia in 1622. The crime was theft. In the more than three hundred years of our subsequent history, the number of citizens put to death by state or federal authorities is approximately twenty-one thousand and growing.

At present in America, the crimes that may result in execution of their perpetrators are first-degree murder, treason, and, in a few jurisdictions, kidnapping and air piracy. In our earlier days—for example, at the time of the country's founding in 1776—in addition to murder and treason, persons could be executed for arson, rape, robbery, burglary, piracy, sodomy, and, in some colonies, counterfeiting, horse theft, or slave rebellion.

The method of choice was hanging. Perhaps we had come some distance from the historical execution methods of flaying, impaling, boiling in oil, crucifixion, burying alive, and similar appalling techniques (though in the United States in the late 1700s some criminals were still put to death by burning them at the stake, pressing them until they were crushed, or drawing and quartering them).

The eighth amendment to our constitution, proscribing the use of "cruel and unusual punishment," caused these particularly gruesome means to be dropped, and hanging remained the executioner's method of choice in America for one hundred years.

Well into the nineteenth century, many of these hangings were public affairs, in order to maximize their purported deterrent effect. In fact, in 1936 in Kentucky, at one of the very last executions to which the public was invited, an audience of twenty thousand persons showed up! Though a Dallas newspaper man in 1977 tried (unsuccessfully) to have an impending execution shown on television, executions in the United States—by whatever means—are now private events conducted before only a few dozen witnesses at most.

Some people opposed to the death penalty argue for throwing them open again as public events in the expectation that widespread revulsion and thus abolition of the death penalty would follow. I suspect that the outcome would be otherwise if the circus-like, souvenir-seeking executions of the last century are any guide.

In any event, whether public or private, hanging was long the method employed. In the late 1880s, however, the Edison Company (proponents of direct electrical current) and the Westinghouse Company (which favored alternating current) were locked in sharp competition for dominance in the electrification of the United States. Edison's competitive campaign included demonstration of the fatal effects on animals of being shocked at high intensities of alternating current. If it could kill animals, they held, it could also kill people. Prison officials of the day were quick to turn this public warning into penological opportunity.

In 1888, the New York State legislature approved the dismantling of its gallows and the construction of the first electric chair, a step the legislation saw as both scientific and humane. That year, in Buffalo, New York, a man named William Kemmler killed his lover Tillie Ziegler with a hatchet, and on August 6, 1890, at Auburn Prison, he became the first man in America to be executed by the electric chair.

The use of the electric chair spread rapidly, and soon it was the preferred method of execution in most U.S. jurisdictions. One exception was the State of Utah, which until 1977 most often employed a firing squad (used in thirty-nine of its forty-eight executions since 1847), in response to the Mormon interpretation of the biblical doctrine of "blood atonement."

Believing that hanging, electrocution, and shooting were too cruel, in 1921 the Nevada legislature passed a "Humane Death Bill," which provided that the condemned person would be executed by lethal gas without warning while asleep in his cell. When, in 1924, the opportunity arose to carry out this mandate, and a no-warning, in-the-cell execution proved unfeasible, the first gas chamber was constructed.

Objecting to all four of these methods on the basis of uncertainty, inefficiency, and cruelty, Oklahoma in 1977 became the first U.S. jurisdiction to carry out the death sentence by intravenous administration of lethal drugs. Then (and now) a combination of barbiturates was used (to put the prisoner to sleep) with a chemical paralytic drug (to stop breathing). Perhaps because of both its appearance of relative humaneness and its low cost, this method of execution is being employed more and more widely across the United States.

So, these are our current choices: hanging, shooting, electrocuting, gassing, and lethal injection.

Hanging causes death by asphyxiation; the person chokes to death. Before losing consciousness, the victim's face often turns purple, his tongue protrudes, his eyes bulge, and he may lose sphincter control. If the ratio of rope length to victim weight is not calculated correctly, decapitation may (and has) resulted.

Death by firing squad is caused by massive injury to vital organs and the resulting hemorrhaging. Though some argue that it is more efficient to fire a single bullet to the head from a pistol at point-blank range (as is currently done in China), Utah (and Idaho) law specifies that a five-man rifle squad be used. Here, four members of the squad are given live ammunition, one is given a blank, and none are told which is which so that none will feel certain he is responsible for the victim's death (though live and blank ammunition recoil differently when fired).

Electrocution has often proven in use to be far less efficient or humane than its original adopters hoped and claimed it to be. Faulty electrodes, voltage intensities set too low for body weight, untrained and highly anxious staff conducting the execution, as well as other difficulties have not infrequently meant long, gruesome, slow, painful deaths punctuated by burning flesh and victim agony.

In the gas chamber, the condemned man is strapped to a metal chair with a perforated seat. A bowl is placed under the chair. Suspended over the bowl is a gauze bag containing one pound of cyanide. The executioner, when ready, lowers the bag into the bowl and, via a tube also under his control, introduces a quantity of sulfuric acid. The acid causes a chemical reaction that slowly releases the poisonous cyanide gas throughout the chamber. As the victim breathes the gas, he may first become giddy. As his respiration becomes difficult, he may panic and, as with the person being hung, he may turn purple, have a convulsion, excrete bodily fluids, and die in agony.

Lethal injection at first sounds better, more humane, less likely to involve error and pain. In practice, it is often a disaster. In recent years in Texas, a frequent user of this method, it took forty-seven minutes for the execution team to insert a usable intravenous line into one inmate; a second was given an incorrect mixture of lethal drugs causing him to choke and heave his way to his death; a third fell asleep (as planned) and then because of inadequate sedation awoke to find himself suffocating; another's IV line sprang a leak, spraying technicians and witnesses with the lethal drugs.

So, folks, those of you out there who favor capital punishment, take your pick. You can hang 'em, shoot 'em, burn 'em, gas 'em, or inject 'em. As for me, no thank you, I'll pass.

Private Ownership of Prison: Pros and Cons

the heavy involvement of private businesses in adult prisons is certainly not a new idea. Convict labor—spinning, baking, nail-making—was done under contract with private entrepreneurs as early as the sixteenth century in European "workhouse" prisons. A hundred years later, many European jails (gaols) were housed in private buildings—castles, market houses—and run by private citizens who had been awarded gaolerships as a sort of pension for faithful service to the king. They charged inmates and their families for lodging, food, tobacco, beer, the right to have visitors; for putting leg irons on, for taking them off; and for any and all other goods, services, and privileges their extorting and exploiting minds could imagine.

Two forms of private business involvement were popular in America's past. In one, the lease system, a private business took over control of the institution, literally leasing it for a fee paid to the government. The business maintained the prison, meted out discipline as needed, and made intense use of the inmates as an (unpaid) labor force. The prison lease system began in Kentucky in 1825 and grew rapidly, especially in the South, after the Civil War, as businesses sought to replace slave labor with prisoner labor. Competitors to such businesses, who, after all, actually had to pay their employees, complained about the unfair competition of the lease system, and it gradually died away.

The contract system took its place, a system that remained in some prisons in the United States until 1940. Here, the state maintained its role as owner of the prison and manager of its daily affairs but contracted with private businesses for work to be done for the contractor but in the prison. Prisoners often were paid a modest wage, and such monies made available to them upon release. Again largely because of organized resistance by competitor businesses, the contract system, too, faded away. Now when product manufacturing goes on within prison walls, the products are usually for state use only. In Auburn penitentiary, a New York State maximum-secure facility in which the contract system first began, instead of the clothing, shoes, carpets, barrels, and horse harnesses of yesteryear, inmates now manufacture furniture for state offices and auto license plates for citizens.

So it can be seen that in one way or another, private businesses have long been involved in either operating prisons or making use of their captive labor force. But leasing, contracting, or even operating are far from the next big step, which we have already begun to take in the United States—private *ownership* of prisons.

At the present time, there are almost fifty privately owned adult correctional facilities in the United States, housing approximately fifteen thousand inmates. Given the strong conservative political atmosphere in our country today, and thus the growing belief that government is too large, expensive, and unwieldy, it is quite likely that the effort to further privatize our prison system will continue and expand.

Numerous other services previously run by local, state, or federal government agencies—building maintenance, garbage collection, bus service, mail delivery—have been taken over by private businesses or other nongovernmental entities; why not our prisons? At the heart of our capitalist system in America lies commitment to the value of private ownership and competition and to the belief that private firms are more efficient and creative than government agencies. So, to repeat, why not private ownership of our prisons?

The arguments for and against are several, varied, and often heatedly presented. Those favoring prison privatization claim that they can both build and run prisons more cheaply yet more efficiently than the government does. We now have a million and a half prisoners locked up in America; with longer sentences being given for more and more crimes, less willingness to release early or use parole as often, the prison population will continue to grow substantially as our country's population grows. Thus, more prisons will be needed. Because they don't have to wait the sometimes two or three years for legislative approval, private firms can build prisons rapidly.

In the typical (state) government-run prison (92 percent of our prisons are state owned), annual operating costs per prisoner average approximately $16,500. The cost in new prison construction per bed is about $75,000 (in maximum secure), $55,000 (in medium secure), and $32,000 (in minimum secure). Privatization advocates claim they can build 'em cheaper and run 'em cheaper. How? Use modular construction; cut out government red tape; use sophisticated management techniques; hire and train fewer staff; use electronic monitoring systems to replace some staff; substitute profit sharing for major fringe benefits to staff; if building facilities in several jurisdictions, purchase materials and supplies at less expense in an economy of scale. Their assertion is that entrepreneurs in any business, including the prison business, are motivated to provide maximum satisfaction at minimum cost.

Government bureaucrats, in contrast, are rewarded not for efficiency but rather by the size of their budget or agency. If they spend less than budgeted, rather than being rewarded as in the business world, they are punished by being allocated smaller subsequent budgets. Finally, this pro view tries to counter concerns of those who claim that business-run prisons are likely to be inhumane and keep prisoners incarcerated as long as possible—because payment is based on a per diem, number-of-prison-beds-full basis—by arguing that liability laws create strong incentives for private firms to run their prisons by providing adequate services in a fair and humane manner.

The other side, those largely against the prison privatization movement, are often the relevant state and federal correctional agencies themselves, their prison employees, and citizens to the left of the political spectrum. What are their arguments?

On ideological grounds, they claim it is both wrong and dangerous to delegate to nongovernment officials the right to carry out state decisions to deprive citizens of their liberty, discipline those citizens when in custody, and use (sometimes deadly) force against them when necessary, such as in escapes or riots. Private corporations are established to generate profits for their owners and stockholders, not serve the public good, and the two goals may often conflict. If instances occur in which there are discrepancies between company policy and government policy, the private prison employee is most likely to be loyal to the side his or her employment bread is buttered on.

In practice, the concern expressed is that inmates may more frequently be abused, neglected, or exploited as fewer and less skilled staff are utilized. Fewer counselors, social workers, teachers, and psychologists may be hired. Vocational, recreational, health care, educational, and other rehabilitation services may shrink or disappear. Worse yet, if workers are getting paid on a per diem basis, discipline reports and accounts of prisoner behavior may be intentionally or unintentionally slanted to negatively influence parole decisions and release dates, or the firm may engage in aggressive political lobbying to influence sentencing legislation so that the average prisoner is incarcerated longer. Further, those against privatization argue, what happens to the prison and the prisoners if the company is sold, perhaps even to a foreign buyer, or goes bankrupt?

The private prison movement in America is still too new for there to be enough solid evidence regarding its costs and effectiveness compared to government-owned and -run facilities. Thus, whether to continue and even expand its growth is still largely a matter of opinion. We have sketched here the main arguments pro and con. What do you think?

6.

violence—reducing solutions

Solutions for Parents

Managing Your Child's Aggression

Raising Children to Resist Violence

the contents of this commentary are drawn from "Raising Children to Resist Violence: What You Can Do," a statement of recommendations based on the work of the American Psychological Association Commission on Youth Violence, of which this writer was a member, and the American Academy of Pediatrics.

Suggestions for Dealing With Children

Give your children consistent love and attention. Every child needs a strong, loving relationship with a parent or other adult to feel safe and secure and to develop a sense of trust. Without a steady bond to a caring adult, a child is at risk for becoming hostile, difficult, and hard to manage.

It's not easy to show love to a child all the time. It can be even harder if you are a young, inexperienced, or single parent or if your child is sick or has special needs. If your baby seems unusually difficult to care for and comfort, discuss this with the baby's pediatrician, another physician, a psychologist, or a counselor.

It is important to remember that children have minds of their own. Their increasing independence sometimes leads them to behave in ways that disappoint, anger, or frustrate you. Patience and a willingness to view the situation through children's eyes, before reacting, can help you deal with your emotions. Do your best to avoid responding to your children with hostile words or actions.

Make sure your children are supervised. Children depend on their parents and family members for encouragement, protection, and support as they learn to think for themselves. Without proper supervision, children do not receive the guidance they need.

Insist on knowing where your children are at all times and who their friends are. When you are unable to watch your children, ask someone you trust to watch them for you. Never leave young children home alone, even for a short time.

Encourage your school-age children and older children to participate in supervised after-school activities such as sports teams, tutoring programs, or organized recreation.

Accompany your children to supervised play activities, and watch how they get along with others. Teach your children how to respond appropriately when others use insults or threats or deal with anger by hitting. Explain to your children that these are not appropriate behaviors, and encourage them to avoid other children who behave that way.

Show your children appropriate behaviors by the way you act. Children often learn by example. The behavior, values, and attitudes of parents and siblings have a strong influence on children. Values of respect, honesty, and pride in your family and heritage can be important sources of strength for children, especially if they are confronted with negative peer pressure, live in a violent neighborhood, or attend a rough school.

Most children sometimes act aggressively and may hit another person. Be firm with your children about the possible dangers of violent behavior. Remember also to praise your children when they solve problems constructively without violence. Children are more likely to repeat good behaviors when they are rewarded with attention and praise.

Parents sometimes encourage aggressive behavior without knowing it. For example, some parents think it is good for a boy to learn to fight. Teach your children that it is better to settle arguments with calm words, not fists, threats, or weapons.

Don't hit your children. Hitting, slapping, or spanking children as punishment shows them that it's OK to hit others to solve problems and can train them to punish others in the same way they were punished.

Physical punishments stop unwanted behavior only for a short time. Even with very harsh punishment, children may adapt so that it has little or no effect. Using even more punishment is equally ineffective.

Nonphysical methods of discipline help children deal with their emotions and teach them nonviolent ways to solve problems. Here are some suggestions:

- Giving children "time out"—making children sit quietly, usually one minute for each year of age (not appropriate for very young children)

- Taking away certain privileges or treats

- "Grounding"—not allowing children to play with friends or take part in school or community activities (only appropriate for older children or adolescents)

Children need to feel that if they make mistakes they can correct them. Show them how to learn from their errors. Help them figure out what they did wrong and how they can avoid making similar mistakes in the future. It is especially important not to embarrass or humiliate your children at these times. Children always need to feel your love and respect.

A positive approach to changing behaviors is to emphasize rewards for good behavior instead of punishments for bad behavior.

Be consistent about rules and discipline. When you make a rule, stick to it. Setting rules and then not enforcing them is confusing and sets up children to see what they can get away with.

Parents should involve children in setting rules whenever possible. Explain to your children what you expect and the consequences for not following the rules.

Make sure your children do not have access to guns. Guns and children can be a deadly combination. Teach your children about the dangers of firearms or other weapons if you own and use them. If you keep a gun in your home, unload it and lock it up separately from the bullets. Never store firearms, even if unloaded, in places where children can find them. Don't carry a gun or a weapon. If you do, this tells your children that using guns solves problems.

Try to keep your children from seeing violence in the home or community. Children who have seen violence at home may be more likely to try to resolve conflicts with violence.

Work toward making home a safe, nonviolent place, and always discourage violent behavior between brothers and sisters. Keep in mind as well that hostile, aggressive arguments between parents frighten children and set a bad example for them.

If the people in your home physically or verbally hurt and abuse each other, get help from a psychologist or counselor in your community.

Sometimes children cannot avoid seeing violence in the street, at school, or at home, and they may need help in dealing with these frightening experiences.

Try to keep your children from seeing too much violence in the media. Seeing a lot of violence on television, in the movies, and in video games can lead children to behave aggressively. As a parent, you can control the amount of violence your children see in the media. Here are some ideas:

- Limit television viewing time to one to two hours a day.

- Make sure you know what TV shows your children watch, which movies they see, and what kinds of video games they play.

- Talk to your children about the violence that they see on TV shows, in the movies, and in video games. Help them understand how painful it would be in real life and the serious consequences of violent behaviors.

- Discuss with your children ways to solve problems without violence.

Teach your children ways to avoid becoming victims of violence. Here are some important steps that you can take to keep yourself and your children safe:

- Teach your children safe routes for walking in your neighborhood.

- Encourage them to walk with a friend at all times and only in well-lighted, busy areas.

- Stress how important it is for them to report any crimes or suspicious activities they see to you, a teacher, another trustworthy adult, or the police. Show them how to call 911 or the emergency service in your area.

- Make sure they know what to do if anyone tries to hurt them: Say no, run away, and tell a reliable adult.

- Stress the dangers of talking to strangers. Tell them never to open the door to or go anywhere with someone they don't know and trust.

Help your children stand up against violence. Support your children in standing up against violence. Teach them to respond with calm but firm words when they see others insult, threaten, or hit someone. Help them understand that it takes more courage and leadership to resist violence than to go along with it.

Help your children accept and get along with others from various racial and ethnic backgrounds. Teach them that criticizing people because they are different is hurtful and that name-calling is unacceptable. Make sure they understand that using words to start or encourage violence—or to quietly accept violent behavior—is harmful. Warn your child that bullying and threats can be a setup for violence.

An Extra Suggestion for Adults

Stay involved with your friends, neighbors, and family. A network of friends can offer fun, practical help and support when you have difficult times. Reducing stress and social isolation can help in raising your children.

Try to make sure guns are not available in your area as well. Volunteer to help in your neighborhood's anticrime efforts or in programs to make schools safer for children. If there are no such programs nearby, help start one!

Let your elected officials know that preventing violence is important to you and your neighbors. Complain to television stations and advertisers who sponsor violent programs.

Parents whose children show the signs listed below should discuss their concerns with a professional, who will help them understand their children and suggest ways to prevent violent behavior.

Warning Signs in the Toddler and Preschool Child:

- Has many temper tantrums in a single day or several lasting more than fifteen minutes and often cannot be calmed by parents, family members, or other caregivers

- Has many aggressive outbursts, often for no reason

- Is extremely active, impulsive, and fearless

- Consistently refuses to follow directions and listen to adults

- Does not seem attached to parents, for example, does not touch, look for, or return to parents in strange places

- Frequently watches violence on television, engages in play that has violent themes, or is cruel toward other children

Warning Signs in the School-Age Child:

- Has trouble paying attention and concentrating

- Often disrupts classroom activities

- Does poorly in school

- Frequently gets into fights with other children in school

- Reacts to disappointment, criticism, or teasing with extreme and intense anger, blame, or revenge

- Watches many violent television shows and movies or plays a lot of violent video games

- Has few friends and is often rejected by other children because of his or her behavior

- Makes friends with other children known to be unruly or aggressive

- Consistently does not listen to adults

- Is not sensitive to the feelings of others

- Is cruel or violent toward pets or other animals

- Is easily frustrated

Warning Signs in the Preteen or Teenager:

- Consistently does not listen to authority figures
- Pays no attention to the feelings or rights of others
- Mistreats people and seems to rely on physical violence or threats of violence to solve problems
- Often expresses the feeling that life has treated him or her unfairly
- Does poorly in school and often skips class
- Misses school frequently for no identifiable reason
- Gets suspended from or drops out of school
- Joins a gang, gets involved in fighting, stealing, or destroying property
- Drinks alcohol and/or uses inhalants or drugs

Tantrums: Kicking, Screaming, and Red in the Face

It's 3:30 in the afternoon, and the young mother is doing some late-day shopping at the supermarket to pick up a few things for supper. Her three-year-old son is sitting in the cart as she hurriedly pushes it toward the store's fruit and vegetable section. By mistake, in her rush, she turns down the cookie aisle. Her son's eyes light up at the prospect. "Cookies," he says, "I want a cookie!" Mom responds, "No, darling, we're going to have supper soon. You can have a cookie later." "No, no, no," he insists, "I want a cookie now!" "You can't have one," mother responds sharply, as she watches his face get red and his arms and legs grow rigid. The escalation rapidly continues, and within a few minutes of louder demanding by the son and refusals by the mother, the child is in a full-blown tantrum—shouting, crying, flushing, arms and legs flailing, kicking anyone and anything in reach.

What is known about such tantrum behaviors? They are so common and so difficult to manage that a better sense of their causes and cures would be useful. Tantrums usually begin between ages one and two, occur in about half of all children, peak in frequency at about age two, and usually are gone by age four or five. The typical tantrum lasts one to four minutes and involves a rapid sequence of four stages:

- **Prodrome.** Although some tantrums seem to arrive "out of the blue," most are preceded by a sometimes lengthy period of whining, irritability, defiant looks, and similar warnings of a storm cloud gathering. This has been called the "rumbling and grumbling" pretantrum arousal stage.

- **Confrontation.** The tantrum proper usually begins with a confrontation between the child and a parent or other individual. A persistent request that has been refused, such as the cookie, seems to light the fuse. Professor Dorothy Evrin at the University of London, an expert on this topic, reports that according to her research, the most common tantrum behaviors are screaming, crying, shouting, hitting, kicking, and flailing. Not uncommonly, during this stage the child may hurt or injure himself or herself and others. The most common source of self-injury is from head banging. Though both boys and girls throw tantrums, hitting and kicking as part of the tantrum is substantially more common in boys.

- **Sobbing.** As the tantrum begins to wind down, sobbing replaces shouting, stillness replaces thrashing, floppiness replaces rigidity. The child starts to regain self-control and to reestablish contact and communication with the parent or other. He or she may, in this stage, even feel guilty and apologize.

- **Reconciliation.** The tantrum ends, often (35 percent) with a cuddle. What about the cookie (or whatever else lit the fuse in the first place)? In 30 percent of the instances, the child does not get its way (no cookie), 6 percent of time, the child does (yes cookie), and about 20 percent of the time, a compromise (cookie later) is the solution. In general, this last tantrum stage is a time of increased contact, communication, and reassurance. Only in about 12 percent of tantrums does the anger and sulkiness persist. Much more commonly, the argument fades away and life goes on as before.

Our example of the struggle over the cookie is probably a good one because the most common issues kicking off tantrum behavior concern eating. Other frequent provocations have to do with confinement (to a stroller or shopping cart), dressing, and similar daily events in which parental and child preferences may clash. Tantrums peak in the late morning (before lunch) and early evening, when the child is likely fatigued.

Tantrums are unpleasant and at times harmful events. It is not easy to do, but if parents or other caregivers can steel themselves and ignore the tantrum behavior, there is a good chance it will become less likely. Psychologists call this *extinction*. Any behavior (including tantrums) that consistently fails to get that valuable reward of attention tends to disappear or extinguish. True, not getting mother's or father's attention will at first result in more, not less, shouting, kicking, and crying. But research shows quite clearly that giving in to the tantrum results in both longer and more frequent tantrums.

Give that reward of attention, instead, to the quiet, non-tantrum behaviors that eventually follow the tantrum. Children who were cuddled (a great form of attention) at this quiet, post-tantrum stage had, in the future, both shorter and less frequent tantrums than did those children who were not.

And remember, be careful next time and don't turn down the cookie aisle!

Television Violence:
What Is a Parent to Do?

television has become our children's master teacher. What are they learning? Because twenty-five violent acts per hour are shown on Saturday morning cartoons and six per hour on evening prime time programming, one thing they are learning about is violence. Some are learning to do it (the copycat effect). Some are learning to be more afraid of their worlds (the increased fearfulness effect). And some are learning to be unconcerned when others are victimized by violence (the desensitization effect).

Research shows that these negative effects of the great amounts of television violence to which our children are exposed are particularly harmful for preschool children, whose critical thinking skills have just begun to develop.

What is a parent to do? Here are some suggestions.

■ Sit down and watch three or four children's shows yourself. As you do, try to *be* your child, see and mentally process the show as he or she would. What is going on? What is make-believe and what is real? What are the shows' lessons about how people get along? About how to solve conflict? About what toys to buy?

■ Don't just flip on the set as you flip on a light switch. Plan the family's TV viewing in advance, and include your child in the planning. Set guidelines together about what kinds of shows, and which particular shows, can be watched, and stick to your selections. As much as possible, emphasize nonviolent shows.

■ Monitor your child's actual television viewing. Help your child understand the unreality of TV violence and its consequences, as well as the undesirability of imitating it. Be sure that what is viewed, and how much is viewed, conforms to the guidelines you have set. A good rule is to limit total viewing to an hour or two each day.

■ If you do fire your TV set as a major baby sitter by limiting the amount to be watched, you'll need to provide your child with interesting alternatives. Games, helping with household chores, and especially reading are some good possibilities. If you feel that more than an hour or two of TV viewing each day is OK, substitute good children's videotapes as alternatives to network or cable programming.

■ Watch some shows with your children, and then talk them over. Find out how they are interpreting what they have seen. Discuss what is real and what is pretend. Make clear your disapproval of the violent acts depicted, and suggest alternative, nonviolent ways the conflict shown could have been dealt with.

Some research shows that only 10 percent of the three to five hours of daily TV viewing by young children is actually children's programming. Ninety percent of what they see are programs designed for adults! This very likely means that much of what your child watches are the programs *you* have decided to watch. Thus, you may do well to change some of your own viewing habits and select violent shows much less often. It will be good for both of you!

■ Pay special attention to the commercials. Some shows are no more than thirty minute "infomercials" for a particular toy or game. Help your child understand those advertiser claims that are exaggerated or false.

■ Do what you can as a concerned citizen to encourage legislators, television networks, and cable companies, as well as advertising sponsors, to substantially increase the levels of nonviolent programming and decrease the heavy diet of violent shows now presented to our children.

Television is a powerful teacher, both for better and for worse, but thus far it is teaching too many of the wrong lessons to our children. Perhaps with enough involvement of all citizens, its potential as a *good* teacher can be more fully realized.

Nonaggressive Children
From Aggressive Environments

for decades, some of the most popular and best supported theories in psychology regarding why people behave as they do have focussed on the individual's environment: family, peer group, media, and so forth. Aggressive behavior, for example, has indeed been shown to grow from overly severe and punitive parenting, association with highly aggressive peers, and heavy viewing of television and film violence. The conclusion is clear: Live with aggressive people (family, friends, media) and there is an excellent chance you too will learn that might makes right and become a chronic aggressor yourself. Such environmental influences on the development of aggression have been found repeatedly in research: in studies of preschool child misbehavior, school violence, juvenile delinquency, spouse and child abuse, and adult criminality.

Yet for every such finding there are exceptions. Some children grow up in highly aggressive worlds, with regular abuse from parents, high levels of peer violence, criminal gang activity and worse in their neighborhoods, and thousands of hours of portrayed violence on their television screens, and still turn out to be well-adjusted, peaceable, productive, nonviolent citizens. One can indeed find good kids in bad places. How so? By what means are such persons, often called resilient children, able to swim against the tide of their angry and violent environments? This is an important question because if what lies behind such nonaggressive resiliency can be identified, perhaps it can also be promoted and disseminated and thus made much more common than it is now. Such resilient, invulnerable, or, as they have also been called, *superkids*, do indeed seem to share certain qualities, qualities that distinguish them from youths who show vulnerability to aggressive environments, not resilience to them. One such quality is the ability to develop a sense of at least some control over important aspects of one's own life, even though so much in one's environment feels out of control and overwhelming.

A second shared characteristic of resilient children and adolescents is that they succeed in at least one thing that is important to them—a craft, a sport, a school subject. One way or another, they achieve something positive that adds significantly to their self-esteem and self-confidence.

A third and perhaps most important quality of youngsters who are able to steer safely through an aggressive world is their success in establishing a positive relationship with at least one significant adult. It may be a coach; a clergyman; a teacher; an aunt, uncle, or grandparent; a cousin or older sibling; a neighbor; or a parent. In this relationship, the adult serves as both a model of positive behavior for the youth and as a source of acceptance, support, and encouragement.

If it works well, such a relationship with a positive adult figure can lessen stress, teach nonviolent coping behaviors, and serve in a sense as a protective envelope helping the youth pass through difficult times and aggressive influences.

If you are or can be in such a relationship with a child or adolescent daily exposed to an aggressive lifestyle, don't underestimate your power to be a positive influence. We all need somebody in our corner, especially in tough times and difficult places—none more so than many of the youngsters discussed here.

Solutions for Couples

*Managing Aggression
in Your Partnership*

Dating as a
Dangerous Game

One hundred years ago, unescorted dating didn't happen. Either two people got together with a chaperone present or one's marital fate was arranged for them and presented to the couple as a settled deal with no dates or other prior meetings between them taking place. As the century progressed, such customs faded, and dating for purposes of socializing, sexualizing, and marriage-scouting became one of our nation's most popular pastimes. Unfortunately, about a third of our dating population report having experienced much less pleasant times during their getting together.

Dates can be times for fun, relaxation, sharing, romance, and other positive experiences. For many, however, dates are punctuated by threats, intimidation, control, coercion, and a broad array of physical abuse. Although both males and females appear to be equally likely to become violent during a date, males are more likely to become aggressive to intimidate, arouse fear, or force unwanted behavior. For them, jealousy, anger associated with sexual arousal, and drinking often seem to drive the abuse. Women, in contrast, seem to grow violent while dating mostly in self-defense or for retaliation. Their motives are often self-protective.

Persons involved in dating violence, whether giving it or getting it, are more likely to come from large urban backgrounds rather than from suburban or rural settings and began dating at an early age, frequently after a childhood in which they themselves were targets of abuse. Younger couples are more likely to be violent than older; couples living together are more likely to be violent than are those living apart. About a third of the couples whose dating includes violence were in similarly aggressive relationships with other persons earlier. Further, if it happens once in a relationship, it is quite likely to happen again.

As is true for homicide, assault, and several other expressions of aggression, reports of date violence are highest in America's Southern states (43.8 percent of couples), next highest in the West (27.5 percent), then the Midwest (25.7 percent), and least in the East (22.8 percent). Males experiencing school, job, or financial problems are more likely than those not undergoing such stress to inject violence into dating experiences. Such violence, in addition, is more likely the longer a couple has been dating or the greater the number of dates they have.

How do most victims respond to such behavior? Only one in twenty-five seeks professional help. About half talk it over with friends or family. If it happens on the first date, according to one study, all of the victims break off the relationship. If it happens after a series of dates, about 30 percent still hang on for better days. Once a couple is living together, or going steady, about two-thirds remain in the relationship, only a third breaking it off. Finally, if engaged to be married and dealt with violently by one's partner, only 11 percent of such persons respond by breaking up.

The hitter will often be contrite, apologetic, pledging better control and better times. Unfortunately, the best predictor of future aggression is past aggression. My advice to targets of such behavior: If you are hit by a date, pack your bags, start your motor, and get ready to split. If you are in a very generous mood and you believe the perpetrator has some especially nice qualities, you may want to stick around for a second date, especially if you can arrange a group date. I strongly advise against it, but you have to set your own risks. However, under no circumstances should you tolerate a second such experience. Your chances of the abuse continuing and maybe even growing worse are great.

Let's Both Calm Down, Then We'll Talk

husband and wife are having an angry argument. Father and son are shouting and cursing at each other and are near to coming to blows. Two drivers, after a near-accident, wave fists in each other's face, screaming threats. Hopefully, each of these angry conflicts can be resolved nonviolently, without physical injury, by means of good communication, assertiveness, negotiation, compromise, or other means. Whichever approach is used, the first step is for both parties to calm down.

To start to reduce your own anger level and combat the rush of adrenalin that causes your heart to beat faster, your voice to sound louder, and your fists to clench, try these methods:

- **Deep breathing.** Take a few deep breaths and concentrate on your breathing.

- **Counting backward.** This is a good distractor from thoughts that keep anger pumping.

- **Peaceful imagery.** Imagine yourself relaxed at the beach, by a lake, or some similar place on a warm and balmy day.

- **Other relaxers.** Try any other thoughts or actions that have helped you relax in the past.

In the final analysis, whenever any of us becomes angry it is not directly because of what anyone else does but rather because of what we say to ourselves, including how we interpret the other person's words or actions. So after you begin calming yourself by the steps listed above, it is time to give yourself certain calming instructions. Try a simple "calm down," "chill out," or "relax." Perhaps you can tell yourself, "I'm not going to let him get to me," or "Getting upset won't help," or "I have a right to be annoyed, but let's keep the lid on." Further self-direction can include benign reinterpretations of what the other person did to provoke you: "Maybe he didn't mean to trip me. He always sits in that stretched-out way." "It's a shame she needs to pick arguments all the time, but its her problem not mine." "No need for me to take this personally."

You'll want to get on with solving the conflict you and the other person are having, so when your self-calming steps are beginning to work, it is time to do what you can to help the other person calm down. Try using as many of the following steps as you can:

■ **Model calmness.** One person's calmness in an argument can really help calm the other person down. Use facial expression, posture, gestures, tone of voice, and words to show you are getting your anger under control.

■ **Encourage talking.** Help the other person explain why he or she is angry and what he or she hopes both of you can do to settle matters constructively.

■ **Listen openly.** As thing are explained to you, pay attention, don't interrupt, face the other person, nod your head, or give other signs that he or she is getting through to you.

■ **Show understanding.** Say that you understand, that you see what the person means. Repeat in your own words the heart of what he or she said to you. Try to let the person know you understand what he or she is feeling.

■ **Reassure the other person.** Point out that nonaggressive solutions to your conflict exist and that you are willing to work toward them. Reduce your threat, inspire a bit of problem-solving optimism.

■ **Help save face.** Make it easier for the person to retreat or back off gracefully. Avoid cornering or humiliating the other person. Don't argue in front of other people. Try to compromise. Make your goal the defeating of the problem, not the other person.

Win-Win Arguing

people argue. Husbands and wives, parents and children, co-workers, strangers. Their arguments may grow in intensity and become abuse, fights, assaults, or worse.

What do they argue about? Slights, misperceptions, insults, sex, money, relationships, drinking, you name it. A key step in preventing and reducing such arguments, as well as the aggression that may go with them, is effective, open, and honest communication between the people involved.

Good communication begins with your intentions. If your goal is to defeat the other person and win the argument, it will be difficult to reduce aggression. If your goal is to join the other person to defeat the problem—what has been called a *win-win strategy*—you've made a good start at likely aggression reduction.

How to get ready for effective, problem-solving communication? Here are some good starting steps:

- **Plan on dealing with one problem at a time.** Seeking to solve an argument with win-win solutions is not an easy task. Don't make matters more difficult by taking on too much at one time. If more than one problem is pressing, take them up in sequence.

- **Choose the right time and place.** Be careful where and when you try to communicate when you or the other person are angry. Avoid audiences; seek privacy. Also, seek times and places in which you are not likely to be interrupted (by people, television, telephone, mealtime) and will be free to finish whatever you start.

■ **Review your plan.** Try to open your mind before you open your mouth. Consider your own views and feelings as well as the other person's. Especially, ask yourself what you can do to bring about a win-win solution to your argument. Rehearse what you and the other person may say. Imagine this conversation in several different forms and outcomes.

Now you and the other person are face to face. Effective problem solvers follow such good communication rules as:

■ **Define yourself.** Explain your views, the reasons behind them, and your proposed solutions as logically as you can. Carefully spell out anything you think might be misunderstood.

■ **Make sense to the other person.** Keep your listener constantly in mind as you talk. Encourage him or her to ask questions, to check out your meanings. Repeat yourself as much as necessary.

■ **Focus on behavior.** When you describe to the other person your view of what happened and what you would like to happen concentrate on actual actions you each have taken or might take. Try to avoid focussing on inner qualities that cannot be seen, such as personality, beliefs, intentions, and motivations.

■ **Reciprocate.** Be certain, as you describe how the other person contributed to the problem and what you think they can do to help solve it, that you are equally clear about your part in both its cause and solution. Be specific, avoid vague generalizations.

■ **Be direct.** Say your piece in a straightforward, nonhostile, positive manner. Avoid camouflage, editing, half-truths, or hiding what you honestly believe.

■ **Keep the pressure low.** To keep matters calm as your problem solving continues, try to listen openly to the other person, offer reassurance as needed, don't paint the other person into a corner, and show that you understand his or her position and plans. If anger and aggression return, take a temporary break and reschedule your discussion for a later time.

■ **Be empathic.** Throughout your discussion, communicate to the other person your understanding of his or her feelings. Even if your understanding is not quite accurate, your effort will be appreciated.

■ **Avoid pitfalls.** Much can go wrong when two people argue, even when they are both seeking positive solutions. There is much to avoid: threats, commands, interruption, sarcasm, put-downs, counterattacks, insults, teasing, yelling, generalizations ("You never . . .

"You always . . ."), not responding (silence, sulking, ignoring), speaking for the other person, kitchen-sinking (dredging up old complaints and throwing them into the discussion), and building straw men (distorting what the other person said, and then responding to it as if they, not you, actually said it). There is, indeed, much to avoid.

Such rules for good, problem-solving communication are easy to present but hard to make use of in the heat of the battle. Nevertheless, if you wish the battle to have a nonviolent, conflict-resolving outcome for both yourself and the other person, they are rules worth following.

Take My Wife—Please

humor is often used to express aggression. A man on the "Oprah" show responded to her question "How would you change your life if you found out you only had six months to live?" by saying that he would move in with his mother-in-law because it would be the longest six months of his life.

In addition to jokes about mothers-in-law, countless ethnic jokes, jokes about bosses, spouses, government bureaucrats, lawyers, and doctors are other examples of aggression through humor. Is it possible that humor can also be used to reduce aggression?

If someone is angry at you, and they believe they have a legitimate complaint or grievance against you, using humor may make matters even worse if it sounds like you are making too light of their anger, not taking them seriously, or even poking fun at them. Yet research does show that under certain circumstances, humor can indeed reduce aggression.

Much of the research on aggression done in psychology laboratories makes use of a device called an *aggression machine*. In its most common use, the research subject sits in one room in front of a piece of equipment (the aggression machine) on the front of which is a row of ten buttons with lights above them. The subject sees a second person (someone actually working for the researcher) go into a second room.

The subject is told he or she is the teacher in the experiment, the other person is to be the learner. The teacher's job is to present material to the learner for the learner to master. Each time the learner answers correctly, the teacher is to reward the person by flashing a signal light, the button for which is also on the aggression machine.

For each error, however, the teacher is to punish the learner by delivering an electric shock. Teachers are told that pressing the first of the ten buttons delivers a mild shock, gradually increasing up to the tenth button, which supposedly gives a powerful jolt. In fact, none of the buttons actually deliver any shock at all, even though subjects participating as teachers regularly believe they do.

Aggression in these research studies is measured by the intensity of the shock delivered (one to ten) and its duration, that is, how long the button was held down.

Of the hundreds of studies of aggression that have used this machine, a number of them have investigated our question here: Can humor be used to reduce aggression? In this research, persons made angry by another individual are given the opportunity to aggress against that person by means of the aggression machine.

Before using the machine, some angered persons are shown neutral pictures (scenery, furniture, art), and some are shown humorous cartoons. Research results were clear: Those shown the cartoons were less aggressive toward the other person (lower and shorter shocks) than were those who saw the neutral pictures.

The one exception to this result is that the opposite has been shown to happen: Humor *increases* aggression when the jokes or cartoons are themselves of aggressive content.

The positive effect of humor on aggression is not only something that happens in a research laboratory. A police officer told me that one day he responded to a domestic dispute call. Upon entering the house, the very upset wife pointed to a closed door and said, "He's in there." The officer kicked open the door she had pointed to only to be faced by the husband with a shotgun in his hands aimed right at the officer. The officer paused a moment, looked the armed husband in the eye, and said, "I've been thinking a long time about taking early retirement, and I think right now would be a great time."

In some combination of laughter and disbelief, the husband put down the shotgun and the incident ended peacefully.

Humor can indeed reduce aggression.

Solutions for All of Us

Managing Aggression in Our Society

Why Is Aggression
So Hard to Change?

for a growing number of American adolescents, aggressive behavior is overlearned, consistently successful, and generously supported by the important people in their lives. Parents, teachers, delinquency workers, and others seeking to change such behavior continue to find it difficult to succeed in doing so with many youngsters. Their first obstacle is the sheer frequency with which the lesson "aggression works" is taught to many youth in our society during their developing years.

Many young people grow up with parents who settle their own disputes aggressively, who frequently employ hitting as a major means of discipline with the youngster himself or herself, as well as with the youngster's siblings; young people play for long periods with aggressive toys used in aggressive games with aggressive peers, they spend thousands of hours playing aggressive video games and viewing televised violence, they may attend a school that uses corporal punishment, perhaps joining an aggressive gang or other peer group.

At home, on the street, at school, in front of the tube, their lives are awash with aggression, which is not only frequent but which also has many of the lesson qualities that promote rapid and lasting learning. It is arousing, it is seen in specific "how-to" detail, it is often carried out by persons the youth admires, and most important, it very often succeeds.

As childhood continues, and as it turns into adolescence, the youth's well-learned lessons become more and more evident in their own behavior. The aggression they have so often seen work for others becomes their own most frequent way of responding.

Aggressive lessons learned well and used successfully will only persist if the important people in the youth's life support such behavior. Unfortunately, such encouragement of the notion "might makes right" is very common—from family, from peers, and from others. In a recent survey comparing chronic fighters with nonfighters in one large American city's secondary schools, 80 percent of the fighters but less than half of the nonfighters said that their families want them to hit if provoked.

Many youths will, in fact, be severely punished and humiliated if they don't use force when parents or others think they should. Similar demands for aggressive action, and praise for its use, is an equally frequent feature of peer group pressure for many youngsters. Such pressure is increasingly apparent both for gang and nongang adolescents, boys and girls alike, and at younger and younger ages.

Having learned well how to be aggressive, found it to be consistently successful, and received generous encouragement and support from important others to keep doing so, chronically aggressive youngsters have a final quality that keeps the nasty behavior going. Stated simply, they don't know what to do instead.

The positive, nonviolent, constructive alternatives to aggression that such a youngster might use instead of a fist or gun are alternatives that he or she has seen too seldom, tried too seldom, and at times been punished for if he or she did make use of them. Hitting the adversary is the means chosen because negotiating, walking away, getting help from an uninvolved adult, making light of the disagreement, and other nonviolent solutions are alternatives rarely seen or attempted by the youth and rarely supported by the other people who are significant in his or her life.

Aggression so often is hard to change because it is taught early, taught often, taught well, supported and encouraged by important others, and seems to be the best and often only alternative for children and adolescents who never really learned otherwise.

But let us be careful in trying to deal with such violence not to place too great a share of the responsibility for its occurrence on the shoulders of the youths themselves. Our shared hypocrisy is that at the same time as we loudly condemn it, so many of us continue to use violence in our homes, streets, schools, and workplaces. We do it, we teach it, we watch it, and we often glorify it. Our words and our deeds need realignment. We must ask no less of ourselves than we ask of our children.

Downsizing Deviance

while completing a review of research and writings on the topic of vandalism recently, I was struck by the manner in which the number of articles published about it grew steadily through the 1960s and 1970s only to drop off to a trickle by the early 1980s. I believe this is a good example of our society's continued downsizing of deviance.

In the early 1980s, drugs, assaults, guns, gangs, and other reflections of high-level aggression grew in frequency in America and with it the amount of public and professional concern. Attention to the lower levels of such behavior—for example, vandalism—correspondingly faded. The criminologists, educators, psychologists, and others who had focussed on and written about vandalism up to 1983 dropped it in order to refocus their efforts on the higher levels of such behavior.

There are many examples of such downsizing in our society today. If you are a smoker and find yourself needing to light up while on a long subway ride in New York City, you can probably do so with little concern for being punished, even if you are sitting below a "No Smoking" sign. The transit police, concerned as they are with assaults, muggings, and other more serious crimes, are in a sense forced to downsize the types of deviance to which they are able to pay attention.

Similar demands for attention to fights, assaults, weapons, and drugs have led the American schoolteacher to progressively expect and frequently tolerate disruptiveness, cursing, defiance, bullying, threats, and rules violations from students. Such downsizing of deviance is a serious matter—often in its own right but especially for what it teaches. Aggression has been shown to be primarily learned behavior. If lower levels of such behavior succeed, are rewarded and not punished, its perpetrators are thus encouraged both to continue it and to escalate its intensity.

The delinquent youth who receives a dozen mere cautions by the family court judge and no negative consequences until his or her thirteenth infraction has learned that deviance is downsized. The acting-up child, whose aggression at home or school is ignored until it approaches peak intensity, has learned that deviance is downsized. So, too, the spray-painting vandal who has tagged much of his or her neighborhood with his or her initials and received only peer admiration for his or her efforts. The adult jaywalker, the driver accustomed to "rolling stops" at stop signs, the neighbor ignoring dog leash laws, and other perpetrators of more minor and now frequently unpunished infractions have each learned a similar lesson.

Low-level deviance, aggressive in particular, needs "upsizing." A number of American city school districts (with more likely to come) have begun carrying out a "zero-tolerance" policy in response to student low-level aggression. You curse, you are automatically (no appeal) out for the day. You disrupt, you threaten, you refuse, you bully: Consequences immediately follow. Research on the effects and effectiveness of punishment reveals that it is the swiftness and certainty of such consequences rather than its severity that primarily determines its effectiveness.

The old saying "You do the crime, you do the time" need not mean the excessively long prison terms currently so popular. More important, the certainty that there will be time that must be served, and the speedy following of such sentencing without undue delay after the crime is committed, appear to be the effective features of punishment. Thus, teachers, parents, and law enforcement officials alike would do well to enact a policy of "catch it low to prevent it high"—and to do so swiftly and without exception.

Gun Control
by Gun Replacement

the often very heated arguments for and against gun control in the United States continue to polarize us, and both those favoring and those opposing such measures are angry and frustrated. Arguments on both sides are repeated endlessly, and little progress toward compromise and accommodation has taken place.

Perhaps a different kind of solution is needed, one that continues the purported advantages of weapons ownership and use but with fewer of its purported dangers, thus satisfying both proponents and opponents. Our suggestion is to legalize, popularize, and encourage sword dueling in the United States.

Guns, of course, are the optimal power tool, the great equalizer, the way to hurt someone badly with minimal risk of bodily harm to oneself. One can shoot from a distance, even while hidden, and certainly beyond arm's reach of the victim. Such advantages to perpetrators helped result in over fifteen thousand gun murders in the United States in 1994.

What would be our likely situation if, somehow, sword use largely replaced gun use by those among us prone to harming others? Popular on and off in several European countries from the Middle Ages to late in the nineteenth century, dueling with swords instead of pulling the trigger of a gun offers several advantages. First, because even if skilled in its use the swordsman is himself at risk of bodily harm, second thoughts might immediately discourage aggression-by-sword. For those duels not denied but actually carried forth, traditional rules dating back to the tenth century would help minimize the number of fatalities. One is that no weapons other than the sword be carried by the participants. Another is that other persons ("seconds") accompany each duelist to prevent such things as ambushes. A third, and most important, is that a successful strike (drawing blood), not necessarily a fatality, ends the duel. There is a winner, there is a loser, both have been brave, face is saved. A puncture wound is better than a bullet wound. Further, once fired, a bullet cannot be recalled, but face-saving dueling can even take place using dull, corked, or sheathed swords that permit winners and losers to be established with no (at least physical) injury to either party.

Unless somehow the seconds or spectators are drawn into the duel, yet a further advantage of swords over guns is that—unlike what is true in many American cities today—bystanders are at minimal risk of being injured or killed.

Less aggression by perpetrators and less harm to participants or to bystanders are not the only benefits should dueling by swords come to replace our love affair with the gun. First, a new organization will likely come into being, the National Sword Association. For those of us not enamored by much that the National Rifle Association seeks to do, perhaps the N.S.A. will, in addition to promoting the joys of dueling, drain off funds and energy from the N.R.A.

Second, if my Freudian colleagues are correct that one of the reasons people own, flaunt, and use guns is to brag that "mine is bigger and more powerful than yours," swords as a replacement weapon and symbol let them boast the even more significant message, "Mine is longer than yours!"

Many American states are now rushing to pass legislation permitting concealed weaponry, particularly the right to carry a handgun hidden from sight. If that right were extended to include dueling swords, it is doubtless likely that some carriers would cut off treasured parts of their own bodies, making the use of even swords for aggressive purposes less likely.

Are there disadvantages to this gun replacement goal? One is the possibility that those favoring and opposing gun control measures will simply shift their pro and con protestations to the use of swords. We risk an era of dueling bumper stickers, those arguing for sword control proclaiming "Swords are for sissies" and the cons "Swords don't kill, swordsmen do."

Differentiations among types of swords may rapidly emerge. Some, such as assault swords (good only for killing, too heavy for dueling) will have to be outlawed, the opponents will claim. Such a step will not take place easily, as the sword control cons will insist that such weapons are protected by the constitution.

Such are the possible advantages and disadvantages of beating our guns into swords. If such a replacement scheme were to go forward, swords and their use must be made more popular. We believe a full-scale campaign can be mounted to accomplish this goal, a campaign that directly mimics the many methods used in America to make guns so popular and admired. Toy swords, sword play games, sword video games, fictional sword heroes on TV ("The Power Duelers") and in the movies (*Return of Zorro*).

Such steps are but a beginning. If we can do anything well in America, it is to sell an idea. Sword use can be sold. Dueling can return. Guns can be replaced. Instead of "Bang, bang, you're dead, " our children, from an early age, can learn to say "On guard!"

Complex Problems
Demand Complex Solutions

In American government, science, business, and elsewhere, an optimistic but misplaced "can do" spirit often promotes the belief that complex problems will yield to simple solutions. Too much use of drugs? Let's declare war on it and get rid of it. Too much cancer? Let's find a magic bullet to wipe it out. Poverty? Again, declare war on it to end it. Welfare costing too much? Workfare will handle that. Other social, economic, medical problems? This, that, or the other program will do the trick.

So too with aggression. Simple prescriptions and their champions abound. More corporal punishment. Less corporal punishment. More fathers in the homes. Less violent television. More Bible instruction. Martial arts training. More police. Wider availability of guns to the citizenry. More gun control. And many, many more.

Yet every act of aggression (as well as each of the social problems we have mentioned) grows from a complex set of sources and has several causes. I frequently give a lecture on why corporal punishment is an in-effective means for changing behavior, a means that helps teach the lesson "might makes right" and thus increases the chances that the youth being punished will become more, not less, aggressive.

On several occasions, a member of the audience has challenged my recommendation against such punishment, saying "I got hit, and I turned out OK." I'm sure most such claims are true because 90 percent of American children are hit by their parents to varying degrees as they grow up and most turn out not to be overly aggressive. But such protestations miss the point. Aggression grows from a complex of causes. One's own punishment history is but one such source. Alone, its contribution may not be enough to yield aggression; in combination with other sources, it may well do so.

So when Johnny smacks Billy, the reasons are usually several and diverse. Some indeed are "in" Johnny. His personality, temperament, self-control, tolerance for frustration, and skills for dealing with provocation are the "scripts" he carries with him for interpreting the behavior of others.

But much of the source of Johnny's aggression lives outside him, often in the sheer presence and behavior of others: criminal behavior by his parents, aggression by the peer group he hangs out with, his heavy diet of television violence. Each of these adds fuel to the potential fire. The presence of weapons and provocation from a possible victim are other external influences upon potential impulses toward aggression.

Complex problems demand complex solutions. Aggression is a complex problem. Our success in its control will be greatest when we deal with both the perpetrator *and* with as many of its "outside" sources as we can.

My own research for many years has focussed on evaluating a method that our center has developed for teaching seriously delinquent youth alternative constructive skills for dealing with frustration and provocation as well as steps for directly controlling their anger. We call the method *Aggression Replacement Training*.

In the studies that we and others have done on this method, our success in teaching such skills, as well as keeping the youngsters from getting back into trouble and being returned to prison, has always been greater when we used the training both for the youths themselves *and* for the important other people in their lives—family, peers, fellow gang members—who often play such a major role in supporting and encouraging the youths' aggression.

Aggression will not be reduced by simple and sometimes simple-minded solutions. Needed, instead, are solutions that match, in their complexity, the complexity of aggression's roots itself.

A Look to the Future

the reflections that make up this book have made it all too clear that aggression in America is with us at high levels and in diverse forms and that it causes great damage to our lives as individuals and as a society. It is *the* major problem facing the United States today.

I would hope, however, that the combined impact of what you have read on these pages does not leave you with a sense of defeat or resignation. Yes, it is true that a great deal of the aggression I have described has been with us a long time, often succeeds in its purpose, tends to be imitated and spread, and thus is difficult, often quite difficult, behavior to change.

Nevertheless, as I look to the future after a professional career of thirty years of working with seriously aggressive individuals, I urge that although it is difficult to be optimistic about where we are heading, we need not be pessimistic. Instead, I believe our best stance is to be realistic. Means for changing aggressive behavior for the better do exist and work reasonably well—if not with the majority of aggressors, at least with a substantial minority of them. These avenues of change come from many fields: psychology, education, sociology, criminology, public health, political science, and more. We certainly have a long way to go, but collectively we are making real progress.

It is work that is most worthy, and it continues . . .